40 Prayers
FOR MY
Future Husband

PREPARING TO RECEIVE
THE MARRIAGE GOD HAS FOR ME

STEPHAN LABOSSIERE

Copyright

40 Prayers for My Future Husband
Preparing to Receive the Marriage God Has for Me

For more information, contact Highly Favored Publishing – highlyfavoredent@gmail.com

Unless otherwise indicated, all scripture quotations are taken from the Holy Bible, New Living Translation, copyright © 1996, 2004, 2015 by Tyndale House Foundation. Used by permission of Tyndale House Publishers, Inc., Carol Stream, Illinois 60188. All rights reserved.

Scripture quotations marked MSG are taken from *The Message*, copyright © 1993, 2002, 2018 by Eugene H. Peterson. Used by permission of NavPress. All rights reserved. Represented by Tyndale House Publishers.

Editor & Creative Consultant: C. Nzingha Smith, SNC2 INK, LLC
Book Interior: A Darned Good Book – www.adarnedgoodbook.com

ISBN No. 978-1-957955-00-1

PRINTED AND BOUND IN THE UNITED STATES OF AMERICA

Dedication

This book is dedicated to every woman who genuinely desires true love in her life, who has ever had to deal with the struggle of dating the wrong man, or not being able to recognize the right one. I know it can get really tough, and my prayer is that every last one of you will be loved, respected, and cherished by the man who is truly best for you.

Author Disclaimer

This book is designed to provide information and motivation to readers. The advice and strategies contained herein may not be suitable for every situation.

Neither the Publisher nor the Author shall be liable for any physical, psychological, emotional, financial, or commercial damages, including, but not limited to, special, incidental, consequential, or other damages as a result of actions taken by the reader.

The fact that an organization or website is referred to in this work as a citation or a potential source of further information is not a direct endorsement of the organization or website. Any information they provide, or recommendations made to individuals are not made by the Author or Publisher.

Further, readers should be aware that the internet websites listed in this work may have changed or disappeared between when this work was written, published, and read.

Every person is different, and the advice and strategies contained herein may not be suitable for your situation. Our views and rights are the same: You are responsible for your own choices, actions, and results.

Table of Contents

Introduction

God loves you. I believe He desires to richly bless you through the union of a happy marriage. As His daughter, you'll need to be prepared for the gift and blessing that is your future husband and a happily ever after in your future marriage.

In order to access the full blessings of God, He requires you to be in relationship with Him. Prayer is not only about communicating your wants and desires to God. It's also about being in relationship with Him. Prayer also helps you build your faith and tap into the power that lives within you. Once you tap into that power, you can use it to change your life.

In this book, I'm going to take you through essentially forty days of praying for your future husband. However, as in all of my books, it's meant to do more than just cover him in prayer. I wrote this book to help you discover yourself and to discover what you'll need to get in order before you're blessed with God's other good thing, your future husband.

Along your prayer journey, you'll be able to get clearer on who you are as a woman. And if you're the type of woman, the type of man you want to marry, wants to marry. If not, this book will help you take steps to become her.

You'll also get clarity on whether or not marriage is for you. Based on what it means according to God's word and intent, not the world's.

Marriage Isn't for Everyone

This is important to point out from the start. The idea of marriage and the reality of being married aren't the same.

We live in a time where too much focus is put on the results of what people have been able to achieve after they've achieved it. Not a lot of light is shone on the process of what it really took for them to get there. This automatically makes most of us want the same results without knowing what it really costs to get them. This is the case with people who have achieved high levels of success in any area, including marriage.

No matter what area a person is successful in, the bottom line is that there was a decision made, a period of preparation, consistent action taken, and processes completed, in order for the person to achieve the results they wanted. We should take this same approach with success where marriage is concerned.

Going through this 40-day prayer journey will help you assess where you are now. After reading it and going through the exercises, it may show you that you're not quite ready yet. This doesn't mean your future husband is unattainable, or a happy marriage is out of reach for you. It just means you'll know what you need to do to become the person who can manifest the blessing of a future husband and a successful and happy marriage. It also might reveal that you are ready and it's just a matter of God's timing.

This book is a hybrid of prayers, coaching tools, introspection, communication exercises, and more prayers. I wrote this book to be very interactive. Faith without works is dead. You need to do the necessary work to go with your prayers in order to manifest your desired results.

You don't need to allow things to just happen to you. You don't have to accept any old thing or person. You are a co-creator, alongside God, in your life. It's time to reclaim your power!

The Right Processes Create Your Desired Results

In this book, we're going to focus on the right processes and not so much on the results. I don't want to dangle a carrot in front of you that will continue to evade your grasp without you knowing it.

Most of the systems set up now are based on this model. They want you to go after what you want, but they don't want you to actually achieve your goals. This keeps you in a vicious cycle of discontent. Operating from a place of discontent means you'll need to fill any sadness or disappointment with whatever it is they want to sell you.

However, I believe if we focus on the work that goes into the results we want to have, we're putting ourselves in a better position to actually reach our goals. If you find out what goes into getting what you want before you work towards it, you can then make an informed decision about whether you really want to spend the time, energy, and resources it'll take you to get it. You'll save yourself from going through all the trouble of trying to get it, only to find out you didn't want it, or it wasn't worth it after the fact.

All it takes is knowing yourself and being honest with *you* about who you are and who you aren't. As well as what you are and aren't willing to do. This will essentially show you what really matters to you outside of it "sounding good" at the moment.

A good example of this is a person who wants a six-pack. The idea of having a six-pack is great. The reality of what it takes to get it and maintain it is another thing. Once the person finds out what it takes to get it, they can be honest with themselves about whether they are willing and able to do the work required to achieve a six-pack. If not, they can decide to be content with working to stay toned and in shape instead.

You might think they're giving up on themselves. They're not. The informed decision is an act of love. They made a clear decision based on honesty, and a sense of self-awareness about who they are, their strengths and weaknesses. They didn't want to be unloving to themselves by setting themselves up for failure to begin with. They empowered themselves by making an informed choice. They didn't waste any vital energy and can be peaceful about their decision. Their energy is then better spent on attaining the goals they set within their own self-knowledge. It doesn't make the goal unattainable or out of reach for them. It brings awareness to what they have to work on. Working on their stamina, self-discipline, and diet more will help them become the person who goes after the six-pack and gets it.

Ask anyone if they want to have a happy and successful marriage and the answer will be, "of course." Then ask a person what they're willing to do and sacrifice to ensure they have a happy and successful marriage. You're unlikely to get a clear or confident answer.

What You Want vs. What You Prepare For

What you want and what you prepare and work for are two different things. One requires no effort on your part. The other will take a dedicated will and decision to do whatever it takes to get the end results you desire.

With manifesting your future husband and creating your happily ever after, I don't want you to be the person wishing and hoping for it. I want you to be fully aware of what it's going to take to achieve it. I also want you to be prepared to create the reality for yourself with God's direction.

This book will not only get you started, but it also provides useful tools for you to use after meeting your future husband. No matter where you are on your journey, I believe it'll be a great resource. Use it during your single and waiting, engaged, or newly married stages of life. You deserve to experience the marriage God has for you and your custom version of a happily ever after.

Let's get started!

Why Pray?

1. Prayer is not only about communicating your wants and needs to God. Prayer also helps to build your faith and tap into the power God has given you as a co-creator. "Faith comes by hearing, hearing by the word of God." Romans 10:17

2. Prayer allows you to speak and hear the word of God. When your words align with God's word, this allows you to receive the manifestation of your prayers.

3. Prayer is also about being in relationship with God and aligning your will to His. Even though God already knows your needs and desires. Prayer is more for you than for the benefit of God. "And without faith it is impossible to please him, for whoever would draw near to God must believe that he exists and that he rewards those who seek him." Hebrews 11:6

4. Being specific in your prayers also matters. Clarity and order are important to God. Praying for someone else changes us in the process. It also humbles us before God as we depend solely on Him for direction in our lives.

5. To "seek God's face" is to strongly desire His presence and blessings. How you posture yourself before God matters as well, along with how you pray.

6. Jesus often prayed for long periods of time alone and when he emerged, he was renewed and filled with power. Modeling Jesus is always the right thing to do.

7. Marriage by God's standards differs from what the world has taught you regarding what marriage is. Praying gives you access to direction on God's version of marriage directly from the Source.

Affirmative Prayers

Have you ever paid attention to how you pray? Most people have a certain praying style. Think about it. Are you used to praying from a place of fear, lack, and unworthiness? Are you used to going to God as a beggar? When you go to God pleading, you usually are still prone to doubt and worry even after praying.

What about praying God's word? If you go to God believing you're His daughter, praying His word, in a posture of expectation with total conviction that your prayers are heard and will be answered, you'll probably feel much different afterward.

Let me be clear. There are many ways to pray and no wrong or right way to do it. However, if you're used to praying to God as a beggar, it's time to upgrade your status.

Now faith is confidence in what we hope for and assurance about what we do not see. Hebrews 11:1, NIV

Affirmative prayer is a form of empowering prayer. The focus is on the desired outcome and not on situational feelings or things. You're not in a posture of begging or pleading with God. Affirmative prayer is also not to be confused with positive thoughts alone. God's Word is living and active and Spirit-filled!

18

By using affirmative prayers you're reminding yourself of the promises God already made to you (building your faith). By praying God's word (scripture), instead of your feelings (which are temporary, fleeting, and not truth), you ensure your prayers align with His will. This way, you can really tap into God's power and blessings for your life.

For the next 40 days, you're going to go before God as his daughter, precious and honored in his sight, with a posture of expectation. You'll pray His word and speak those things to come as though they are already. This way you can be prepared to receive the future marriage God has for you and the happily ever after you actually desire.

You're that powerful. It's time to own your power and believe, without doubting. You are worthy of the love, and many other gifts God intended for you to have, even before He formed you in the wound.

How to Use This Book

A couple of things about how to use this book.

• You need to set aside a block of time that is uninterrupted and free of distractions for your prayer time and the exercises. Earlier in the day usually works best.

• You'll also need a dedicated journal to use to complete the various exercises throughout the book.

I created a physical journal, *My Time Journal* with this in mind. Go to mytimejournal.com to get your copy. You might be able to go deeper when you actually write out your thoughts. But, if it's easier to take notes on an electronic device, do what works best for you. Just turn the device on airplane mode during your dedicated prayer and reflection time so you stay focused.

As you read, focus on growth in these seven areas:
1. Growing closer to God.

2. Establishing a consistent prayer life, which is important for your overall life and your future marriage.

3. Learning patience and how to let God be God.

4. Building your faith and starving your fears and worries about being single and/or married.

5. Practicing loving communication so it's easier and more natural for you when you get into a relationship with your future husband.

6. Expanding your love vocabulary. This builds your confidence when expressing yourself because you'll have the right words to say no matter what the situation is.

7. Developing more emotional intelligence. It's the ability to be aware of, control, and express your emotions and is important to the success of all your relationships in life.

Talking Points & Insight Pages
At the end of each section, I've included a page for you to note things you might need to work through, or revisit later to gain clarity on after you complete a set of prayers.

Think about who you might want or need to discuss these talking points with. Then be intentional about having the necessary conversations to work through the concerns with the chosen person. If it's God, this would be in your own prayer time. If it's with a trusted friend or professional, you'll need to reach out to them and schedule time.

Depending on where you are on your journey, your future husband may or may not be in your life currently. If he is, schedule an hour a week to work through the insights and any other talking points that need to be discussed.

God Controls the Timing

Let me pause here and remind you that God controls the timing. It's important to remember *this book is a tool of preparation and encouragement and not a guarantee* that you'll receive your future husband at the end of the 40-day prayer journey.

However, I am confident that at the end of this prayer journey, you'll be in a much better and more prepared state to receive him and work alongside him to create a beautiful relationship and future marriage together.

You'll have increased your self-awareness, worked through some of your kinks, experienced a deeper level of healing, and feel more optimistic about your ability to custom-create your happily ever after because you'll really know what that truly means for you.

You don't attract what you want. You attract who you are.

Loving Expression Exercises Explained

Y ou form a habit by repeatedly doing something. Repetition is the only way to get good at anything. You have to practice that thing repeatedly until it becomes natural and intuitive.

I want this to be the case in your ability to communicate to your future husband clearly and lovingly, no matter what. Loving communication doesn't only apply to your needs being met. It also applies to you using your words to praise, edify, uplift, support, and express your love to and for him openly. Doing so will help you practice continually trusting him with your vulnerability in the process.

No special occasion needed. It needs to be standard practice.

No relationship is all roses and sunshine 100% of the time. This being the case, you'll also need to practice using loving communication to correct him or communicate when things aren't working or about things that need improvement.

Since unloving communication is the current standard in our relationships, these practices will help you prepare to use loving words even when you may have an attitude, or he's done or said something to make you angry.

There'll also be times when you need to admit you hurt him or made him angry and will need to own up to it in order to move forward. This is where you'll also need to practice taking responsibility, not getting defensive, and actually be able to apologize for your actions in a loving way.

Unfortunately, it's unavoidable to get on each other's nerves, push boundaries, buttons, and cause hurt and pain at some or multiple points within your relationship. However, in order to move forward, loving communication is even more important. It'll help ensure the problems don't persist or worsen by unloving communication in the moment. It takes practice to maintain a loving nature instead of blowing up and risking destroying things further in the process.

You've heard the phrase, "practice makes perfect." Well, perfection isn't our goal here. Our focus is on improving your skill of loving communication and helping you develop it before you need to use this skill in your future marriage.

Doing these exercises will also help you further by bringing up any past issues that still need to be healed. They'll help you build up your love vocabulary and allow you to get intimate with yourself. These exercises are also designed to help you identify the ways you need to be loved and the types of things you value.

This is vital information to know because you'll need to teach your future husband how to love you in ways that actually make you *feel* loved. If you don't know yourself or how you need to receive love in order to feel loved, then how can you teach him? Impossible, right? Exactly.

So, while you're praying and covering him throughout this 40-day prayer journey, you'll also be learning things about yourself that'll help you forge a closer bond with him by raising your level of self-awareness. Your words can either uplift and edify or tear down and cause brokenness, hurt, and pain.

Be a woman who knows how to soothe and mend by letting sweet words (honey) drip abundantly from your lips into his heart. You'll connect with him in ways you never even imagined possible by speaking into his life lovingly.

As always, stay open to the process. Any resistance you may feel is a sign the process is working; you just need to trust it and persist. Remember: It's all for your highest good.

Why Do You Desire Marriage?

B efore you get started praying for your future husband, it's important you start the journey knowing your "why." Doing so will help you measure the growth you'll experience as you read. You'll be able to compare who you are now to who you will be at the end of your 40-day prayer journey.

Why do you want to get married? Why do you desire a husband? What about marriage excites you? What are some things that you're willing to give up in order for your marriage to thrive and be successful? Are you ready to put in the work required for you to fully prepare to receive the marriage God has for you and create your happily ever after?

Take some time out now in your dedicated journal to reflect and see what answers come up for you. This is without a doubt some of the most important insight you'll need to learn about yourself. Especially if you've never asked yourself these types of questions about marriage before.

What you find are your truest motivations for one of the most important decisions of your life may surprise you. If any of your reasons for wanting to be married or desiring a husband come from outside of yourself and are based on other people's lives or input, you're probably not ready to be married yet.

Spend some time getting clear about the way you think about what it means to actually be married to someone else.

No matter what your current motivations are, be prepared to come out of this journey, a changed woman. In order to do that, you'll need to have the courage to throw away what you thought you knew about marriage, including any previous expectations and everything else that doesn't align with God's *word* and *will*. You'll also need to be brave enough to face yourself.

Remember to give yourself the gifts of grace and forgiveness as you travel along. Be kind and gentle with yourself. Judgment doesn't have a place on this journey. It's not about right or wrong. It's about discovering truth and changing unfruitful behaviors, so you're aligned properly going forward.

It's okay to not know. We all have been taught by the second-hand experiences of other people. This doesn't make them right. It also doesn't mean that we can't choose differently for ourselves and for our lives now.

"Don't copy the behavior and customs of this world, but let God transform you into a new person by changing the way you think. Then you will learn to know God's will for you, which is good and pleasing and perfect." Romans 12:2

Are you ready to die to your old self? It's time to find out.

Scripture Meditation #1

*"O Lord, hear me as I pray; pay attention to my groaning.
Listen to my voice in the morning, Lord. Each morning I bring
my requests to you and wait expectantly."*
Psalm 5:1-3

1

His Mind

*D*ear Heavenly Father, I pray over my future husband's mind. Let him cast all of his anxieties and fears on you because you care for him. God, if any doubts fill his mind, let your comfort give him renewed hope and cheer. Keep him in his right mind. Give him clarity of thought to make sound and wise decisions over his life, finances, health, and relationships.

Your word says, "Set your minds on things above, not on earthly things." What he focuses on produces the quality of his life. I pray that he safeguards all the different gates in which information enters his awareness. I pray he is always on guard to immediately reject that which does not serve his highest and best good.

Rid his mind of all distractions and sources of discouragement. Clear out anything that would cause him a disconnect with you.

Help him keep his thoughts and mind focused on your word and higher things that are true, noble, right, pure, lovely, admirable, excellent, and praiseworthy. Help him remember to think about such things. When he focuses on these things and your teachings and has put them into practice in his life, your peace will be with him.

Lord, let my future husband fix his eyes not on what he sees, but on what is unseen. Remind him that what is seen is temporary, but what is unseen is eternal.

God, thank you! I believe you've heard my prayer and will honor it. By faith and the power of the Holy Spirit's intercession with me, I declare it done and so, Amen.

Scripture References:
I Peter 5:7, Psalm 94: 19, Colossians 2:2-3, Philippians 4:8-9, II Corinthians 4:18, Romans 15:5-6, Matthew 18:20

2

Self-Acceptance

*H*eavenly Father, I pray you'll give my future husband the ability to accept himself just as you created and fashioned him to be and just as Christ accepted him, in order for him to bring praise to you, God.

May he honor your design and plan for how you saw best to construct him from the inside out. So that he values and takes care of the body and mind you blessed him to inhabit and use. I pray he doesn't misuse, abuse, or underutilize himself. He is his most valuable asset.

He is your creation. I pray he accepts himself with love and patience as you continue to develop and fashion him into the man you desire him to be. May he be able to realize his true potential and fulfill his purpose for being in life.

Help him be a good steward of himself as an act of love and devotion, reciprocating your love for him back to you. In doing so, he'll know how to show the same love outwardly in the world, in all of his relationships—including our future marriage—and as a foundation to sustaining our happily ever after.

Self-acceptance is the foundation for self-love. God, I pray my future husband owns all of who he is, both the light and the shadows. May he seek counsel in the Holy Spirit and in your word for his ongoing validation and to confirm and affirm his true worth.

God, thank you! I believe you've heard my prayer and will honor it. By faith and the power of the Holy Spirit's intercession with me, I declare it done and so, Amen.

Scripture References:
Romans 15:7, Ephesians 4:2-6, Matthew 18:20

3

Self-Esteem & Confidence

*H*eavenly Father, I pray my future husband's self-esteem and confidence is healthy and stable. I pray it's rooted in who you created him to be as a man and in your word, God.

Plant your word in his heart, so he measures himself by your standards and not the standards of this world. I pray his self-talk is uplifting, edifying, and grounds him in a place of faith, truth, positivity, and love.

Fix his thoughts and focus on who you designed him to be, so that he knows who he is and whose he is at all times. Especially as he encounters life's difficulties and many challenges.

May the words he uses to describe himself be words that confirm to him his value and worth in the areas that matter most to you. You desire him to be patient, humble, tolerant, kind, and gentle, which is true power under control.

May he know in his heart and carry in his spirit your deep love, adoration, and care for him. I pray he operates in this world from a place of self-respect and not from self-loathing. That he holds his head up level at all times and his body language communicates the highest view of self without a trace of arrogance or conceit.

If he's endured life experiences that have damaged his healthy and Godly self-view, I pray your grace and healing over the attacks on his confidence and esteem.

Give him a Spirit of discernment around any habits that weaken his healthy self-view and worth so he can make any needed adjustments and align with what's best and highest for his life.

May you continue to help him fortify his inner resources and how he sees himself as your son.

God, thank you! I believe you've heard my prayer and will honor it. By faith and the power of the Holy Spirit's intercession with me, I declare it done and so, Amen.

Scripture References:
Romans 12:2, Daniel 2:21

4

Wisdom

*D*ear *Heavenly Father*, thank you for giving wisdom to those who seek you. I pray you'd bless my future husband with your divine wisdom. Let him not forget your words or turn away from them. Though it cost all he has, may he get understanding.

Lord, I pray my future husband trusts you with all his heart and does not lean on his own knowledge. May he hold tight to your instruction, not letting it go; and guarding it well, for it is his life.

Do not allow him to see himself as wise in his own eyes or deceive himself and think he is wise by the standards of this world either. For the wisdom of this world is foolishness in your sight, God. Your word says, "He catches the wise in their craftiness. The Lord knows the thoughts of the wise are futile. Whoever restrains his words has knowledge, and he who has a cool spirit is a man of understanding."

I pray my future husband knows the benefits of having a cool spirit and accepts your correction and guidance over him because you discipline those you love. Your wisdom from above is first pure, then peaceable, gentle, open to reason, full of mercy and good fruits, impartial, and sincere.

God, thank you! I believe you've heard my prayer and will honor it. By faith and the power of the Holy Spirit's intercession with me, I declare it done and so, Amen.

Scripture References:
Proverbs 3:5, 4:5-7, 13, I Corinthians 3:18-20, Hebrews 12:6, James 3:17, Proverbs 17:27-28

5

Inner Peace

*D*ear Heavenly Father, I pray my future husband knows what it's like to be clothed and protected by your peace that surpasses all understanding.

I pray he doesn't allow his heart to be troubled nor afraid by anything or anyone because he knows your peace is a refuge for him when he seeks you and goes to you in prayer and with a spirit of humility.

In John 14:27, it says, "Peace I leave with you; my peace I give to you. Not as the world gives, do I give to you. Let not your hearts be troubled, neither let them be afraid."

I pray your peace fills my future husband to overflow. Cause him to experience lasting joy in every area of his life as he leans on and trusts you. God, you are the source of true peace, hope, and joy. May he always look to you as his Source and use this knowledge to realign anytime life knocks him down or tries to convince him otherwise.

Don't let him be fooled or misguided by the falsehoods of this world and the lies or opinions of others that would try to manipulate or control his actions, thoughts, and ways of being.

God, thank you! I believe you've heard my prayer and will honor it. By faith and the power of the Holy Spirit's intercession with me, I declare it done and so, Amen.

Scripture References:
Philippians 4:6, John 14:27, John 14:1

6

God's Will & Life Vision

*D*ear Heavenly Father, your word says, "'For I know the plans I have for you. Plans to prosper you and not to harm you, plans to give you a hope and a future." Thank you for calling my future husband out to be one of your chosen people.

Reveal your vision and will for his life to him as he seeks your face daily. Help him be open to hearing your call. When you call him, I pray his response is to listen and obey.

Give him an eager heart to do your will. Bless him with a spirit of obedience and the humility of a servant leader. Help him stay focused on your will and vision for his life so that he can experience success in everything he does.

I pray the Holy Spirit will correct his thoughts and actions when they don't align with your will or vision for his life so that he doesn't get too far off track and miss or block his own blessings.

Please counsel him on how to carry out the plans and the work that is a part of his life's purpose. Strengthen my future husband's faith so he can continue to press forward according to your instructions, even when he is fearful, tired, or discouraged.

Tune his hearing so he hears your voice the loudest, above all the noises of distraction. I pray he has a spirit of holy boldness and that he will always have the courage to do and say the things you give him to share with others through his work and gifts.

Allow miracles, signs, and wonders to be normal and regular occurrences in his life. I pray he is sensitive to the Spirit and can perceive all the blessings you bring his way, intended to help him realize his full potential and assist him on his journey.

God, thank you! I believe you've heard my prayer and will honor it. By faith and the power of the Holy Spirit's intercession with me, I declare it done and so, Amen.

Scripture References:
Jeremiah 29:11, I Samuel 3

Coming in Agreement Prayer

*M**ay you, God*, who gives endurance and encouragement, give my future husband and I, the same attitude of mind and heart toward each other that Christ Jesus had toward us, so that with one mind and one voice we may glorify you.

I pray that upon our meeting we will begin our union and sustain it through an unconditional acceptance of the individuals we are and as we join to become one in love and marriage.

As an extension of his and my own unconditional self-acceptance, may we too, as a unit, learn to accept one another as you accept us. In order to continue to bring praise to you, God. May we conduct ourselves with all humility, gentleness, and patience as an act of worship to you.

In Jeremiah 17:7-8, it says, "But blessed are those who trust in the Lord and have made the Lord their hope and confidence. They are like trees planted along a riverbank, with roots that reach deep into the water." I pray my future husband and I will always put our hope, trust, and confidence in you so that we always have your blessings follow us in all we do.

41

I pray we always attempt to protect the unity of the Spirit with the peace that ties us together through both unconditional acceptance and unconditional love that we can only find through our relationship with you, God.

Heavenly Father, I pray that you, the source of hope, will fill us completely with joy and peace because we trust in You. Then we will overflow with confident hope through the power of the Holy Spirit.

God give us eager hearts to do your will. Give us spirits of obedience and the humility to be servant leaders. First to one another, then to others in our lives, and in all other areas we have influence. Help us stay focused on your will and vision for our lives as individuals and also as one body so we can experience success in everything we do.

May the desires of our hearts be in alignment with your will for us and our future marriage.

God, I pray your wisdom from above rains down on us as a unit. It is first pure, then peaceable, gentle, open to reason, full of mercy and good fruits, impartial, and sincere. I thank you for granting wisdom to those who seek it out. God, together we seek your guidance and wisdom for the benefit of us both.

Your word says, "where two or more gather together in your name, you are there with them." I come in agreement with my future husband now as we cover ourselves in prayer.

God, thank you! I believe you have heard my prayer and will honor it. By faith and the power of the Holy Spirit's intercession with me, I declare it done and so, Amen.

LOVING EXPRESSION #1

—

Praise

Your future husband has just miraculously read your mind and without you asking him or instructing him, somehow, he just knew what you needed at that moment and took action to get it done. You're smiling. Stress-free. Safe and taken care of. You feel special and fully loved by his actions.

Part 1: Written Love Note

Now, take your dedicated journal and write your future husband a love note praising him, so he knows you value what he's done and how it made you feel.

What kind of action(s) would cause this kind of praise and the feelings I mentioned above?

Go into detail about what you'd say to him. Use pet names if you like. Include how you'd react to the situation physically. What would your body language be like? Would you go to him and openly show him your affection? Would he get a big kiss or hug? If the action turns you on, let him know that too. Let it play out in as much detail as possible. Experience it in your mind's eye as real.

Here are some phrases you can use to get you started thinking about how you'd like to express yourself and what you'd like to say in your own words in your praise love note.

Loving Expressions

Thank you, my love.	I adore you.
You're so considerate.	Your caring shows.
I appreciate your actions.	I'm grateful for your love.
You read my mind.	I love you, loving me.
You make me better.	You make my heart smile.

Part II: Spoken Love Note

After you've written your love note praising him for hitting the mark, take your letter and read it out loud as if you're speaking directly to your future husband. Imagine that he's there, standing or sitting in front of you. Visualize the experience and feel all the feelings you might feel in the moment.

If you get choked up, allow it. If tears of joy come, let them. The purpose is to really have the experience in advance so it's something you can get comfortable doing, feeling, and experiencing repeatedly. Until it's more natural.

Things to Remember

#1: Smiling will help you really make the feelings more real.

#2: Visualization and spoken word are both powerful manifestation tools to create and bring the things you want into existence.

#3: Men like to know when they've done something right! It encourages us to repeat that action again and again so we can continue to reap the good benefits it provided.

Everyone has a need to be valued and appreciated in the moment. So, yes, it's a BIG deal to make sure he hears *your* praises!

Selah {Pause}

Before you continue, I want you to pause here. Check in with yourself. How are you feeling? How has this first group of prayers changed how you're thinking about your future husband as a human being and the things he might deal with in life and in his personal walk with God?

How difficult or easy was it for you to write and speak praises to him? How did you feel thinking about this playing out in real life? Did you get carried away daydreaming?

Now go back through the previous group of prayers and pray them over yourself. Change out the pronouns he, him, etc. Put me, myself, and I in their place. Focus on the below themes.

Your Mind
Self-Acceptance
Self-Esteem & Confidence
Wisdom
Inner Peace
God's Will & Life Vision

STEPHAN LABOSSIERE

Take some time and reflect on where you are in your walk with God. How can these parts of your character have a positive or negative effect on your relationship with your future husband and in your future marriage, if not properly developed?

"The energetic messages we emit to the universe
are reflected back to us in how we pray."
Anekia Nicole

Talking Points & Insight

Use this space to note things that came up for you that you want to work through or revisit later to gain clarity or peace on.

Talking Points for You & God:

1.

2.

3.

Talking Points for You & a Trusted Friend or Professional:

1.

2.

3.

Talking Points for You & Your Future Husband:

1.

2.

3.

Insight Gained

_____

_____

_____

_____

_____

_____

_____

_____

_____

Scripture Meditation #2

*"Keep on asking, and you will receive what you ask for.
Keep on seeking, and you will find. Keep on knocking, and the
door will be opened to you. For everyone who asks, receives.
Everyone who seeks, finds. And to everyone who knocks, the
door will be opened."*
Matthew 7:7-11

7

His Health

*D*ear Heavenly Father, I pray for my future husband's complete health and well-being. I pray he knows his body is a temple of the Holy Spirit within him, and that his temple is a gift from you.

Help him realize he is not his own, for you bought him at a high price. May he learn to glorify you, God, in and with his body. I pray you'd fill him with joy, which is good medicine for anything that might ail him.

I pray you'd give him a spirit of discernment so he can fully understand his body's intelligence and workings. Help him tune into this higher intelligence and be more inclined to follow and listen to its guidance above all else.

I pray his body is in alignment with your will for it. I pray my future husband knows how to be fully present in his body and can enjoy and honor it properly.

I cancel and come against any dis-ease that might want to live in his body. I call it out and speak wholeness over him. God, help him make good decisions about what he puts into his body daily. I pray he is knowledgeable in preventative health measures so he can enjoy a fruitful and long life.

God bless my future husband with great health all the days of his life. I pray that all may go well with him, even as his soul is getting along well.

God, thank you! I believe you have heard my prayer and will honor it. By faith and the power of the Holy Spirit's intercession with me, I declare it done and so, Amen.

Scripture References:
1 Corinthians 6:19-20, Proverbs 17:22, 3 John 1:2

8

His Heart

Heavenly Father, thank you for giving my future husband a heart that remains teachable. Your word says, "as water reflects a face, so a man's heart reflects the man." I pray my future husband's heart reflects a man who is after your own heart.

Teach and guide him in Your ways so that he'll walk in your truth. Give him an undivided heart; not entertaining both good and evil. Let my future husband stand firmly and correctly in goodness. Your word says, "A good man brings good things out of the goodness of his heart, and the evil man, evil things out of his heart."

Lord, you search the heart and examine the mind to reward a man according to his conduct, according to what his deeds deserve. Search my future husband's heart, test him, and know his thoughts. See if there is any offensive way in him. Convict him in any areas where he needs to grow gentler, more loving, kind, humble, or repentant.

When you test him and the road gets hard, don't let his heart be troubled. Prove yourself to him so his trust in you may be established, further purifying his heart by faith.

Help him set his heart on things above, where Christ is, seated at your right hand, God. I pray he keeps his heart with all vigilance, for from it flows the springs of life.

I pray he'll have a forgiving heart. Help him not to see forgiveness as being weak. Grant him the wisdom and understanding that forgiveness is for his own benefit and betterment in life. Keep his heart from hardening and letting bitterness or distrust overtake him, as these don't produce more love, but cuts love off from taking root and growing within him.

I pray he is open to emptying his heart before you, so it's not weighed down by troubles, pain, or heartbreak. Restore wholeness from any heartaches he's experienced, so these things won't hold him back from being open to receiving your love and his own.

Your grace is sufficient for him, and your power made perfect in his weakness. I pray he has a deep relationship with you and trusts you completely. As a result, he can be vulnerable in your presence. Cradle him in your loving arms and hold him in perfect peace, always.

God, thank you! I believe you have heard my prayer and will honor it. By faith and the power of the Holy Spirit's intercession with me, I declare it done and so, Amen.

Scripture References:

Proverbs 27:19, Psalm 86:11, Luke 6:45, Jeremiah 17:9-10, Psalm 139:23-24, John 14:1; Acts 15:9, Colossians 2:1-4, Proverbs 4:23

9

A Kind & Caring Spirit

Heavenly Father, I pray my future husband has a kind and caring spirit. I pray his actions and the intentions behind his actions support his highest good, always, so that he is constantly adding blessings to his life.

Your word says, "A man who is kind benefits himself, but a cruel man hurts himself." Allow my future husband to be a recipient of the kindness he shows to others. Allow him to be uplifted. Let his kindness and heartfelt intent be received well by others, always seeking to pay him back in kind.

May he possess, as one of your chosen sons, holy and beloved, a compassionate heart, kindness, humility, meekness, and patience so that things will go well with him all the days of his life.

I pray he's naturally considerate and thoughtful without needing to attach an expectation to his actions. I pray he is caring and knows how to nurture himself and others in ways that convey care and respect.

Anytime he feels depleted, show him how to look to you for refreshing and replenishment because you are the true Source.

Your word says, "Whoever pursues righteousness and kindness will find life, righteousness, and honor." I pray your kindness and favor leads him to repentance.

God, thank you! I believe you have heard my prayer and will honor it. By faith and the power of the Holy Spirit's intercession with me, I declare it done and so, Amen.

Scripture References:
Proverbs 11:17, Colossians 3:12, Romans 2:4, Proverbs 21:21

10

His Courage

Dear Heavenly Father, I pray my future husband possesses divine strength and unshakeable courage. Help him not to be afraid or panicked when faced with the tests and trials of life. Go before him and neither fail nor abandon him.

Teach him the importance of being courageous as a follower of Christ, and in his faith walk. Help him realize that having courage doesn't mean the absence of fear and that being afraid is not a sign of weakness. Fear is a guide and can be a teacher and motivator if discerned properly.

Grant him the wisdom to know the difference between real and perceived threats to his physical, mental, emotional, and spiritual well-being. Teach him how to trust in you completely because he won't always be able to see his way through. But he will make his way through anything because you are with him.

"Have I not commanded you? Be strong and courageous. Do not be frightened, and do not be dismayed, for the Lord your God is with you wherever you go."

Just like you commanded Joshua to be strong and courageous, I pray my future husband knows you are with him wherever he goes. May he find strength in knowing you are with him always, no matter what.

May a spirit of peace clothe him because he puts his confidence in you and leans on you for guidance and strength in his times of difficulty.

Your word says, "Wait on the Lord: be of good courage, and he shall strengthen thine heart: wait, I say, on the Lord."

I speak patience and calmness over my future husband in times of anxiety, high stress, and testing. I pray he has a spirit of perseverance and determination to help him pursue, overtake, and recover all you have for him, for your glory and his highest good.

God, thank you! I believe you have heard my prayer and will honor it. By faith and the power of the Holy Spirit's intercession with me, I declare it done and so, Amen.

Scripture References:
Deuteronomy 31:6, Joshua 1:9, Psalm 27:14, I Samuel 30:8

11

Physical Protection

*D*ear *Heavenly Father*, I pray my future husband puts on your full armor of protection every day so that he's equipped to carry out the plans you have placed on his heart and purposed for his life.

God, allow my future husband to go on his way safely and for his feet not to stumble. Cover him with your feathers. Shelter him with your wings. Your faithful promises are his shield and security.

Even though he walks through the valley of the shadow of death, may he fear no evil, for you are with him; your rod and your staff, they comfort him all the days of his life.

God, I pray for protection over any spiritual or psychic attacks that try to come up against him daily. I pray my future husband knows how to pray in the Spirit at all times and on all occasions in order to fortify his hedge of protection spiritually, physically, mentally, and energetically.

I pray for complete protection over him, and everyone connected to him, as he stays committed to your plan and vision for his life. Thank you for keeping him in everything.

Help him to discern the things that are within his control and those that are outside of it. May he protect himself from the habit of being weighed down with burdens, worries, and troubles that are not his to carry. May he have the wisdom to surrender everything over to you because you love and care for him.

God, thank you! I believe you have heard my prayer and will honor it. By faith and the power of the Holy Spirit's intercession with me, I declare it done and so, Amen.

Scripture References:
Ephesians 6:11, Proverbs 3:23, Psalm 91:4, Psalm 23:4, Ephesians 4:31, II Corinthians 12:9

12

A Healthy Sense of Humility

Heavenly Father, I pray my future husband knows the rewards for humility and fear of you are riches, honor, and life. I pray he understands the true definition of humility, which is freedom from pride and arrogance and not a low self-view. Humility also doesn't require him to have low self-esteem or to be a doormat for others to walk over him.

You reward those who humble themselves before you by exalting them in due time. May my future husband not grow impatient with waiting on your divine timing and take his life in his own hands. Obedience outweighs sacrifice and I pray he stays obedient to your will and guidance.

May those who scorn your name or are far from you see the good in my future husband through his acts of humble service, making you appealing to all. May he find validation in you and not try to seek it out in the world.

God, you oppose the proud and give grace to the humble. May your grace rest upon my future husband as he seeks to live his life with all humility and gentleness, with patience, and bearing with everyone in love.

Give him a spirit of obedience and the humility to be a servant leader first to himself, then to others in his life, and in all other areas he has influence. Heavenly Father, thank you for your favor, grace, and mercy, which are new and available to him every day.

God, thank you! I believe you have heard my prayer and will honor it. By faith and the power of the Holy Spirit's intercession with me, I declare it done and so, Amen.

Scripture References:
1 Peter 5:6, Proverbs 22:4, James 4:10, Ephesians 4:2

Coming in Agreement Prayer

Heavenly Father, your wisdom grants us well-being, prosperity, safety, and health to our bodies. I pray we'll always use higher wisdom when making decisions concerning every area of our health and well-being. Renew our minds and correct our beliefs about what's best for having a long life full of high energy and optimal health.

God, you know our hearts. Clear out anything not like you. Create in us clean hearts and renew a right spirit within us. God, we want to learn to love you first with all our hearts, minds, and souls. We won't create idols for ourselves, including each other. Help us remember you're the Source of everything. You gifted us to each other to be resources and as physical expressions of your love for us.

Help us be kind and compassionate to one another, forgiving each other (constantly), just as Christ forgave us. I pray we'll work at getting rid of all bitterness, rage and anger, habits of fighting and being disrespectful, along with every form of meanness that lives in our hearts because of past hurts or learned behaviors from our previous environments or relationships. I pray we learn how to feel safe in your and each other's love.

God, grant us the courage to be who you created us to be and to live out of a place of authenticity in our future marriage. I pray we will always put our hope, trust, and confidence in you so we're able to experience your blessings flow in our lives.

Give us the courage to face any challenging or insurmountable obstacles that try to come up against us. Give us the courage to reject any outside influences in our future marriage that don't align with your word and direction for our lives. We trust you completely. You know what's best for us.

I pray we never forget your teachings. I pray we'll both maintain sound judgment and discretion; they will be life for us, an ornament to grace our necks. Then we will go on our way in safety, and our feet will not stumble.

With full humility, God, I pray my future husband and I will learn to regard our marriage with the utmost importance. I pray we regard our future marriage more highly than our individual lives. Cover us with your grace and teach us how to be completely gentle, kind, and patient with each other in love, always, and through all things.

Your word says, "where two or more gather together in your name, you are there with them." I come in agreement with my future husband now as we cover ourselves in prayer.

God, thank you! I believe you've heard my prayer and will honor it. By faith and the power of the Holy Spirit's intercession with me, I declare it done and so, Amen.

LOVING EXPRESSION #2

Compliments

Your future husband is wearing something you find sexy and attractive. Maybe he just came from the barber, and you love the look of his fresh haircut and tapered beard or clean-shaven face. He might be sweaty from finishing an intense workout and you've watched his body transform and can see his hard work paying off.

Maybe he has a habit you love or something else you want to give him a compliment about. You feel very attracted to him on all levels at this moment.

Part 1: Written Love Note

Now, take your dedicated journal and write your future husband a love note complimenting him. Maybe he does one thing really well or it can be for something he's wearing, his body, looks, mind, thoughtfulness, etc. Complimenting him lets him know you value these things, have taken the time to notice, and you want to share how you feel about him.

What things would cause you to want to compliment him and have you feeling the ways I mentioned above?

Go into detail about what you'd say to him. Use pet names. Include how you would react to the situation physically. What would your body language be like? Would you go to him and openly show your affection? Would he get a big kiss or hug? If the action turns you on, let him know that too. Let it play out in as much detail as possible. Experience it in your mind's eye as real.

Here are some phrases you can use to get you started thinking about how you'd like to express yourself and what you'd like to say, in your own words, in your compliment-filled love note.

Loving Expressions

Wow! I'm in awe of you.	I admire you.
You're brilliant.	I love your beautiful mind.
Thank you for being.	Hey handsome.
You have a special way...	Your body is everything.
I love your smile.	You are remarkable.

Part II: Spoken Love Note

Now that you have your words together and know what you want to say to shower him with compliments and show him you pay attention to and desire him. I want you to take your letter and read it out loud as if you were speaking directly to your future husband. Imagine he's there, standing or sitting in front of you. Visualize the experience and feel all the feels you might feel in the moment.

Allow yourself permission to be you. If you feel flirty, cool. If you're shy or observe that you have reserves, no worries. You can explore this more later. The purpose of this is to really have the experience in advance so that it's something you can get comfortable doing, feeling, and experiencing, until it's more natural for you.

Things to Remember

#1: Smiling will help you really make the feelings more real.

#2: Visualization and spoken word are both powerful manifestation tools to create and bring the things you want into existence.

#3: Men like to get compliments too! We want to know that we're desired by our woman. He needs to know you're paying attention to him. Your compliments help to build up his self-confidence and to know that you value his efforts to get better, grow, and take care of himself. It gives him more fuel to keep going and lets him know he's on the right track.

Again, compliments encourage men to repeat the actions that reap them more good benefits. Everyone needs to be valued and appreciated in the moment. So, yes, it's a BIG deal to make sure he knows you like how he looks, thinks, behaves, and that these things attract you and cause you to desire him physically!

Selah {Pause}

Pause here. Check in with yourself. How are you feeling? What things came up for you during this set of prayers? How was completing the second loving expression exercise?

How has this second group of prayers changed how you're thinking about your future husband as a human being and the things he might deal with in life and in his personal walk with God?

Now go back through the previous group of prayers and pray them over yourself. Change out the pronouns he, him, etc. Put me, myself, and I in their place. Focus on the below themes.

Your Health
Your Heart
A Kind & Caring Spirit
Courage
Physical Protection
A Healthy Sense of Humility

Take some time and reflect on where you are in your walk with God. What shape is your heart in currently? What about your physical, mental, and emotional health? What areas would you like to develop the most from the above list? Rank them in order of importance, with 1 being the highest priority to 5.

"Love is a universal language, and everyone
benefits from learning to speak it freely."
C. Nzingha Smith

Talking Points & Insight

Use this space to note things that came up for you that you want to work through or revisit later to gain clarity or peace on.

Talking Points for You & God:

1.

2.

3.

Talking Points for You & a Trusted Friend or Professional:

1.

2.

3.

Talking Points for You & Your Future Husband:

1.

2.

3.

Insight Gained

_____

_____

_____

_____

_____

_____

_____

_____

_____

Right Intentions, Not Based Upon Lack

Having the right intentions before you begin anything is vital to its success. This is especially true when you're talking about creating a union before God with another soul for the rest of your life.

If you're looking for someone to fill the voids in your life, you're not ready to be married. If you feel you're at a certain age and "should be" married already, you're probably not ready to be married. If you're only focused on the ceremony, the type of dress you want, and who will be in your wedding party, guess what? You're not ready to be married.

I can't stress this point enough. Make sure you have the right intentions for *why* you want to be married and *why* you desire a husband. Make sure lack is not the root of those intentions.

Lack is the state of being without or not having enough of something. If your intentions are based on a perception of lack, you're going to start your marriage off in a deficit. The meaning of deficit is inadequacy in amount or quality.

You'll be setting your future husband up to run a race, he'll lose. As a result, you'll doom your future marriage from the start. Why? Your expectations of what marriage is and who he is "supposed" to be as your husband, will not be met. Plain and simple.

More than likely, you'll feel entitlement instead of gratitude for him and the marriage. This will play out in how you treat him and the marriage. You might not be thankful and appreciative of him or his efforts. Why? Because you won't value them. Starting things off from behind, subconsciously, will make things never seem like they are enough. The marriage, or him for that matter, will never truly satisfy you.

Rooting your desires in any lack will deprive you of starting things off on the right foot and only continue "the hurt people, hurt people" cycle.

It's not your future husband's job to live up to expectations or responsibilities that are not his to fill.

You have a responsibility to yourself for yourself. It's up to you to create the life and love (of Self) you truly desire *first*. This way, when he's added to the equation, he'll be adding to the healthy foundation you've already built. The union can then thrive, grow, and continue to flourish, all while being able to endure the elements that will come along to test it. It all starts by building on truth and a solid base of genuine intentions.

"Anyone who listens to my teaching and follows it is wise, like a person who builds a house on solid rock. Though the rain comes in torrents and the floodwaters rise and the winds beat against that house, it won't collapse because it is built on bedrock. But anyone who hears my teaching and doesn't obey it is foolish, like a person who builds a house on sand. When the rains and floods come and the winds beat against that house, it will collapse with a mighty crash." Matthew 7:24-27

You want to build your future marriage on solid rock and not sand, so it can withstand the tests of time. When you do things right from the start, you rarely have to rebuild from scratch later on.

Scripture Meditation #3

"This is the confidence we have in approaching God: that if we ask anything according to his will, he hears us. And if we know that he hears us — whatever we ask — we know that we have what we asked of him."

I John 5:14-15

13

His Work

*D*ear Heavenly Father, allow your favor to rest on my future husband. Establish the work of his hands. I cancel any attacks of the enemy seeking to destroy or sabotage his efforts. May he find honor and respect in his life, his work, and his relationships.

Your word says, "And whatever you do, in word or deed, do everything in the name of the Lord Jesus, giving thanks to God the Father through him. Whatever you do, work heartily, as for the Lord and not for men, knowing that from the Lord you will receive the inheritance as your reward."

Bless the works of his hands with not only wealth but also a sense of satisfaction and deep fulfillment. I pray my future husband experiences extreme joy and contentment from his work and the use of his many gifts, skills, and talents.

Shower him with favor. Bless him to receive fair payment for his work and other contributions to his employer or clients if he has a business. Help him focus on the larger vision of serving and doing everything for your glory and honor and not the approval or validation of men.

STEPHAN LABOSSIERE

Help him not to equate his worth with his work. He is much more than what he does to earn money for a living. Help him establish his own definition of success. I pray you'd empower him to act on the things that bring him the most joy and satisfaction and not chase after meaningless things he doesn't value for the sake of seeking other's approval.

Lord, open the heavens, the storehouse of your bounty so my future husband may lend to many nations but will borrow from none. Lord, make him the head, not the tail. If he pays attention to the commands you give, God, place him always at the top, never at the bottom. May he serve you all the days of his life.

God, thank you! I believe you have heard my prayer and will honor it. By faith and the power of the Holy Spirit's intercession with me, I declare it done and so, Amen.

Scripture References:
Psalm 90:17, Colossians 3:17, 23-24, Deuteronomy 28:12-14

14
—

Contentment

*D*ear Heavenly Father, I pray that a lasting spirit of contentment cover, and act as a sanctuary for my future husband to dwell. Help him identify his wants from his needs. Grant him the wisdom to realize what is enough for his own happiness and exact goals so that he is in a constant state of fulfillment.

I pray he's able to feel the pleasure of what it's like to be at ease and content with himself, where he is in life, and what he has. Your word says, "Take care, and be on your guard against all greediness, for one's life does not consist of the abundance of his possessions."

Help him resist the need to chase fantasies and material gains meant to keep up appearances and control him in worldly culture. These things lead to greed, envy, scarcity mindset, and unhappiness. Cleanse him of any habits of comparison because it kills off joy and sows seeds of discontent, creating blocks for true connection.

This doesn't mean he won't aspire to growing and evolving, but he'll be doing so from a healthy place instead of a place of lack, low values, and a spirit of competitiveness.

Your word instructs, "he can do all things through Christ that strengthens him." Help him see and believe in this truth, no matter what his current situation is or what is ahead of him. I pray you would teach him how to be content in all situations and that he will put his trust in you above all else.

Instruct him on the things that matter to you and what he should value over anything else. So, he can invest his time, energy, and resources in these things in order to see them mature and grow and to reap the bounty you have prepared specifically for him and those connected to him.

Give him the courage to decide for himself what he wants and how he'll be most fulfilled and content in life, so he has a healthy way to measure his pursuits now and going forward.

God, thank you! I believe you have heard my prayer and will honor it. By faith and the power of the Holy Spirit's intercession with me, I declare it done and so, Amen.

Scripture References:
II Corinthians 2:10, Luke 12:15, Philippians 4:13

15

—

Emotional Intelligence & Maturity

Dear Heavenly Father, bless my future husband with a high level of emotional intelligence and maturity. I pray he has the awareness and ability to understand his own emotions. I also pray he possesses the self-control to manage them.

As an emotionally mature man, I pray he doesn't view emotions as weakness. Instead, I pray he values his emotions. So he doesn't shy away from or hide how he feels or become uncomfortable when others express their feelings to him.

Teach him how to be angry without sinning; and to not let the sun go down on his anger, so he won't give any opportunity to the devil to take a foothold in his heart.

I pray for protection against all toxic emotions he may deal with including anger, resentment, unforgiveness, hatred, fear, stress, guilt, and shame that would cause him to harden his heart and turn away from you, God.

Your word says, "Get rid of all bitterness, rage and anger, brawling and slander, along with every form of malice."

Reveal to him the healthiest ways he can move through, express, and release any toxic emotions from his emotional, mental, physical, and energetic bodies.

I pray he's able to replace any toxic feelings within his emotions with peace, love, and a spirit of ongoing forgiveness.

God, thank you! I believe you have heard my prayer and will honor it. By faith and the power of the Holy Spirit's intercession with me, I declare it done and so, Amen.

Scripture References:
Ephesians 3:16-21 & 4:31

16
—

True Strength

*D**ear Heavenly Father*, teach my future husband that true strength is trusting you to fight his battles. It's living by your word and being led by your Spirit. It's him humbling himself and allowing you to lead as the head of his life. It's him living a life where he's patient, loving, tolerant, kind, and gentle, which is really power under control.

"Not by might, nor by power, but by my Spirit, says the Lord of hosts."

May he behold you, God, as all-powerful. May he trust you, and not be afraid of any situation, thing, or person; for you are his strength, song, and salvation. You are for him so there is no one that can be against him and win.

"I pray ... also that the eyes of your heart may be enlightened in order that you may know ... his incomparably great power for us who believe. That power is like the working of his mighty strength, which he exerted in Christ when he raised him from the dead..."

Help my future husband to know that it's not by the strength of the body, will, or mind that one prevails. Those who stumble will be armed with strength. It's you, Lord, who humbles and exalts. Everything happens in your divine timing and everything works out for our good and the good of those who love you.

God, thank you! I believe you have heard my prayer and will honor it. By faith and the power of the Holy Spirit's intercession with me, I declare it done and so, Amen.

Scripture References:
Zechariah 4:6, Ephesians 1:17-20, Psalm 27:1,
Romans 8:28, 31

17

Trustworthiness

Heavenly Father, I pray my future husband is a trust-worthy man, dependable, honest, and reliable. God, sanctify him in the truth; your word is truth. I pray he knows he is accountable to you in all his words and deeds. So that even in private, he acts with integrity and takes right action when no one else is watching.

Your word says, "One who is faithful in very little is also faithful in much, and one who is dishonest in very little is also dishonest in much." I pray my future husband is faithful in little so that you see what he's done in secret and reward him openly with favor, wealth of every kind, and expanded influence.

You've taught him regarding his former way of life, to put off his old self, which is being corrupted by its deceitful desires; and to be made new in the attitude of his mind; and to put on the new self, created to be like God in true righteousness and holiness.

Because he trusts you with everything concerning his life, I pray my future husband follows your ways and example of how to walk and live his life in true righteousness and holiness by your grace.

God, thank you! I believe you have heard my prayer and will honor it. By faith and the power of the Holy Spirit's intercession with me, I declare it done and so, Amen.

Scripture References:
John 17:17, Luke 16:10, Ephesians 4:22-24, Matthew 6:4

18

Spiritual Maturity

Heavenly Father, just as my future husband received Christ Jesus as Lord, continue to give him the desire to live his life upright. Let his roots anchor in the truth of your word so he can build a solid foundation to stand on. Help his faith grow strong so he will overflow with thankfulness.

When he was a child, he talked like a child, thought like a child, and reasoned like a child. Now that he is a man, give him the wisdom and discernment to recognize any childish ways he still operates in, and put them behind him. May he continue to grow and mature in his spiritual walk every day of his life.

I pray he considers the consequences of his decisions and actions prior to making them and will seek your wise counsel so he may be successful in everything he does.

Your word says, "But solid food is for the mature, who because of practice have their senses trained to discern good and evil." I pray my future husband knows how to discern good and evil and will reject those things that aren't from you, God.

I pray he's not tossed back and forth by the waves and blown here and there by every wind of teaching and by the cunning and craftiness of people in their deceitful scheming. Instead, I pray he'll speak the truth in love, and will grow to become in every respect the mature body of him who is the head, that is, Christ. From him, the whole body, joined and held together by every supporting ligament, grows, and builds itself up in love, as each part does its work.

"For this reason also, I have not ceased to pray for him and to ask that my future husband may be filled with the knowledge of His will in all spiritual wisdom and understanding, so that he will walk in a manner worthy of the Lord, to please Him in all respects, bearing fruit in every good work and increasing in the knowledge of God."

God, thank you! I believe you have heard my prayer and will honor it. By faith and the power of the Holy Spirit's intercession with me, I declare it done and so, Amen.

Scripture References:
*Colossians 2:7, I Corinthians 13:11, Hebrews 5:14,
Ephesians 4:14-16, Colossians 1:9-10*

Coming In Agreement Prayer

Heavenly Father, I pray you'll bless my future husband and I with new ideas and the ability to work together in creating wealth. Bless the works of our hands. Bless us in our careers and in our work as stewards of your Kingdom for your glory and honor always.

God, you know our hearts. Give us the courage to decide for ourselves what we want and how we will most be fulfilled and content in life. I pray we have a healthy way to measure our pursuits now and going forward. Help us be satisfied and thankful for what we have, including each other. Teach us how to set boundaries around our time so we aren't sacrificing precious time and energy on things that don't bring us any lasting joy or fulfillment.

I pray we'll both use self-control to manage our emotions and wisdom and patience in order to understand them. I pray as a couple we will value each other's emotions and not shy away from or hide how we feel or get uncomfortable when the other expresses their feelings. Teach us how to express our feelings in a loving and respectful manner, no matter what.

God, true strength is trusting in you completely and letting you fight our battles. It's living by your word and being led by your Spirit. It's humbling ourselves and allowing you to lead as the head of our lives. Grant us the grace to be patient, loving, tolerant, kind, and gentle in everything we do and how we interact with each other, ourselves, and our community.

God, I pray we'll both choose to discard our former lives and ways of living and put off our old selves, which were being corrupted by deceitful desires. Renew our minds. I pray we'll put on new identities in Christ, created to be like you in true righteousness and holiness. I pray we both live in honesty, truth, and integrity with each other. Make us both dependable and reliable, doing what we say we will do, always.

God, give us the wisdom and discernment to recognize any childish ways we still operate in and the courage and strength to put them behind us. I pray we continue to grow and mature in our spiritual walks more every day. Help us to be more like you and to desire the things of your heart. I pray we will walk in a manner worthy of pleasing you, Lord.

Your word says, "where two or more gather together in your name, you are there with them." I come in agreement with my future husband now as we cover ourselves in prayer.

God, thank you! I believe you've heard my prayer and will honor it. By faith and the power of the Holy Spirit's intercession with me, I declare it done and so, Amen.

LOVING EXPRESSION #3

Encouragement

Your future husband has just received notice that he might get laid off at his company. He has doubts about securing another position in his field this late in his career. Perhaps he's up for a promotion and he's feeling unsure of himself and whether he has what it takes to get it.

He might have a dream of owning his own business and has been carefully planning his strategy to launch it. However, now that he's so close, he's sabotaging his efforts.

You're supportive. Things are stable financially.

The communication is open. Although there's a lot of uncertainty, overall things are good.

Part 1: Written Love Note

Take your dedicated journal and write your future husband a love note encouraging him, so he knows you not only believe in him, but that you also think highly of his worth, skills, and capabilities.

What kind of mindset would you need to have to express this kind of encouragement given the uncertainty and other feelings I mentioned above?

Go into detail about what you'd say to him. Include how you would react to the situation physically. What would your body language be like? Would you go to him and openly show him your affection? Would he get a big kiss or hug? Would you suggest some cuddle time? Let it play out in as much detail as possible. Experience it in your mind's eye as real.

Here are some phrases you can use to get you started thinking about how you'd like to express yourself and what you'd like to say in your own words in your encouraging love note.

Loving Expressions

I believe in you.	I support you.
We're a team.	How can I help?
You can do anything.	Let's pray about this.
You're favored by God.	You're not alone.
I trust you.	Faith over fear, baby.

Part II: Spoken Love Note

Now that you have your words together and know what you want to say to encourage him for whatever situation he's facing, take your letter and read it out loud as if you were speaking directly to your future husband. Imagine he's there, standing or sitting in front of you. Visualize the experience and feel all the feelings you might feel in the moment.

Whatever emotions or natural reactions you have, allow them. I want you to get comfortable doing, feeling, and experiencing encouraging him, until it becomes natural to you.

Things to Remember

#1: This is an opportunity for you to flex your nurturing muscles as a woman. However, it'll only be possible if you don't see your gift of nurturing as a weakness. You'll need to connect to your own feminine energy in a healthy way in order to use it.

#2: Men need a lot of encouragement and reassurance. It may not appear to be the case, but trust me, we don't always have it all figured out. Depending on a man's level of maturity and his own level of self-awareness, he may not know how to communicate his pain points or areas of insecurities. It'll just show up in his behavior instead. However, this is where you come in as his future wife. He needs to know that you can pour encouragement into him when needed and won't view him as weak or less than because of it.

#3: Knowing how to pour into your future husband this way will establish an irreplaceable bond between the two of you.

So, yes, it's a BIG deal to encourage him and make sure he knows that it's safe for him to not know what to do sometimes and for him to be human and not superman!

Selah {Pause}

Pause here. Check in with yourself. How are you feeling? What things came up for you during this last set of prayers? How was completing the encouraging expression exercise? Did you experience any blocks while writing your note or saying it?

How has this third group of prayers changed how you're thinking about your future husband as a human being and the things he might deal with in life and in his personal walk with God?

It's time to go back through the previous group of prayers and pray them over yourself. Change out the pronouns he, him, etc. Put me, myself, and I in their place. Focus on the below themes.

Your Work
Contentment
Emotional Intelligence & Maturity
True Strength
Your Trustworthiness
Spiritual Maturity

Take some time and reflect on where you are in your walk with God. Which above areas are you strongest in? Which areas do you still need to develop? Remember: judgment has no place here. You're learning more about yourself and the only way to do that is to ask the right questions for deeper awareness.

> "Awakening is not changing who you are
> but discarding who you are not."
> Deepak Chopra

Talking Points & Insight

Use this space to note things that came up for you that you want to work through or revisit later to gain clarity or peace on.

Talking Points for You & God:

1.

2.

3.

Talking Points for You & a Trusted Friend or Professional:

1.

2.

3.

Talking Points for You & Your Future Husband:

1.

2.

3.

Insight Gained

_____

_____

_____

_____

_____

_____

_____

_____

_____

Scripture Meditation #4

*"Pray in the Spirit at all times and on every occasion.
Stay alert and be persistent in your prayers for
all believers everywhere."*
Ephesians 6:18, NLT

19
‒‒‒‒‒

His Friendships & Family Ties

Dear Heavenly Father, bless my future husband with friends that are like iron. Let them sharpen each other and build each other up in wisdom and strength. I pray his friends don't deceive him because bad company ruins good morals. May he surround himself with friends who refuse to gossip, harm their neighbors, or speak evil about their friends.

Help him restrain from seeking quantity over quality. Because your word says, "A man of many companions may come to ruin, but there is a friend who sticks closer than a brother."

Bless my future husband with proper discernment regarding choosing his friends wisely and having the courage to walk away from friendships that keep him from living out your will for his life.

Teach him how to be a good friend to others and not self-seeking based on what others can do for him. I pray he knows how to show appreciation and care for his close friends, so they feel valued and loved by him.

Within his own family, I pray he operates in harmony and love. I pray he receives unlimited support and acceptance of who he is within his circle of friends and within his family. I pray there is a sense of unity within all of his relationships and that respect and unconditional love are at the center of them.

Help him recognize love from manipulation and control within his family dynamic. Bless him with peace regarding any relationships that need to be cut off if they have a negative impact or keep him in bondage. Because you made him new in you.

Break any bonds built on deceit, blame, shame, or guilt. Teach him how to love at a distance if needed.

Show him how unconditional love and acceptance feel so he has an accurate way of measuring how others should treat him. I pray he's established healthy boundaries around his heart and can teach people how he needs to be treated and loved.

I pray his family is encouraging, respectful, and loving toward him and his decisions in life. I pray for harmony over discord. May he honor his mother and father regardless of the health of the relationship so that he may live a long life and find unlimited favor with you, Lord.

God, destroy any soul ties he created prior to giving his life to you and being saved.

Your word says, "Christ's love controls us. Since we believe that Christ died for all, we also believe that we have all died to our old life. He died for everyone so that those who receive his new life will no longer live for themselves...So, we have stopped evaluating others from a human point of view...This means that anyone who belongs to Christ has become a new person. The old life is gone; a new life has begun!"

God, thank you! I believe you have heard my prayer and you will honor it. By faith and the power of the Holy Spirit's intercession with me, I declare it done and so, Amen.

Scripture References:
Proverbs 27:17, I Corinthians 15:33, Psalm 15:3, Proverbs 18:24, Proverbs 18:24, Ephesians 6:2-3, II Corinthians 5:14-17

20
—

Deep Insecurities

Heavenly Father, I pray you'd heal any feelings of insecurity or instability within my future husband. Root out the negative causes of these unhealthy emotions that overwhelmingly shape his self-image and influence his behavior.

Heal any deep insecurities within him resulting from instabilities caused as a child while he was in the care of others. Reshape any distorted view he has of himself or his place in the world because of these false beliefs.

I pray a renewing over his mind. Correct any false teachings projected onto him from his past. Right any wrong thinking he's developed regarding his beliefs about his ability to be loved, safe, protected, and cared for in his life by other people.

Clear out any critical and judgmental thoughts he has about himself that are negative and self-defeating or cause him to stumble on his walk with you.

Reveal any blind spots within him causing destructive thoughts which fuel these insecurities so he can work on these areas of brokenness. I pray for the restoration and wholeness of his healthy self-esteem and belief in himself, and his abilities to be successful, loved, safe, and prosperous in his life.

Your word says, "But you are a chosen race, a royal priesthood, a holy nation, a people for his own possession, that you may proclaim the excellencies of him who called you out of darkness into his marvelous light."

God, reveal to my future husband the evidence of your unwavering love and the power of your living word that's present and working in his life. Soften his heart so it's not callous and causing him to miss out on the daily miracles present in his life. Help him forget the former things so he can enjoy the new things you want him to experience in his present and future moments.

God, thank you! I believe you have heard my prayer and will honor it. By faith and the power of the Holy Spirit's intercession with me, I declare it done and so, Amen.

Scripture References:
1 Peter 2:9, Romans 12:2

21

Healing Past Traumas

Dear Heavenly Father, I pray for divine, supernatural healing of my future husband's past traumas. Help him work through any ongoing, troubling reactions, or suppressed emotions resulting from living through one or continuous traumatic experiences.

I pray my future husband will pray without ceasing and pour out his heart and soul to you, God. Help him to deal with the things that trouble him the most, deep inside. May he cast all his cares on you because you care about and love him unconditionally. He is safe in your presence and covered by your grace.

I speak against any feelings of denial, shame, guilt, depression, misplaced or internalized blame, hopelessness, damaging emotions, destructive relationship patterns, fear, anger, rage, emotional cutting, self-hatred, numbing, self-harm, nightmares, insomnia, body aches or tremors, bad memory, or any other physical, emotional, or psychological wound that is the result or symptom left over from the original trauma(s). As these keep him feeling separate and distant from experiencing your and other's love for him.

Reveal to him the emotional wounds in need of healing. Bless him with the tools he needs to work to release them and heal from them, so they don't show up as sickness in his body or mind over time.

Transform all his triggers—that seek to take him back to the incident(s) and that cause him to relive the pain, hurt, and trauma all over again—into powerful tools and testimonies of your power working in his life. Strengthen his belief in your ability to work everything out for his good and the good of those who love you.

Bless him with the strength to face his past traumas with courage and a spirit of forgiveness for his own benefit and release, so he won't cause himself constant unnecessary suffering.

Teach him how to surrender his pain to you and let go of the need to hold on to that which doesn't serve him, including trying to make sense of the senseless actions of others. I pray my future husband learns to depend on you, God, to right the wrongs of others where he is concerned.

Your word says, "For our struggle is not against flesh and blood, but against the rulers, against the authorities, against the powers of this dark world and against the spiritual forces of evil in the heavenly realms."

You heal the brokenhearted and bind up their wounds. God, apply your healing balm to each injury and the damage it caused him. Breathe into him your breath of new life and re-store him to wholeness in you according to your original design.

Your word says, "No weapon that is fashioned against you shall succeed, and you shall refute every tongue that rises against you in judgment. This is the heritage of the servants of the Lord and their vindication from me, declares the Lord."

God, thank you! I believe you have heard my prayer and will honor it. By faith and the power of the Holy Spirit's interces-sion with me, I declare it done and so, Amen.

Scripture References:
I Peter 5:7, Psalm 147:3, Isaiah 54:17, Matthew 10:29-31, Romans 8:28, Ephesians 6:12

22

—

Healing Feelings of Unworthiness

Heavenly Father, I pray my future husband knows he is worthy, valuable, and more than good enough as he is. I pray his early childhood experiences helped to enforce these fundamental values within him. I pray he was seen and accepted for who he is and feels secure in that as a man.

Your word says, "Are not two sparrows sold for a penny? Yet not one of them will fall to the ground outside your Father's care. And even the very hairs on your head are all numbered. So don't be afraid; you are worth more than many sparrows."

I pray my future husband knows in his heart that he is valuable beyond measure. If he didn't have an early foundation in life, of security, acceptance, unconditional love, and a sense of him being valued, I now stand in the gap for him.

God restore my future husband's ability to believe in himself. Allow him to see himself as you created him to be. Not the way he was taught or conditioned to see himself by those caring for him throughout his life, or from his community, culture, or society if the influences are unhealthy.

These projections are not his truth. Your word is truth. I speak your word over the scars left by any mishandling of his feelings, his body, or by him feeling invisible or not worthy of care.

Before he was formed in the womb, you knew him, and before he was born you consecrated him; and set him apart as your own. You purposed his life and knew the plans you had for him, plans for good and not for evil, to give him a future and a hope.

Restore any hope and vitality he's lost from enduring hardships in life that have added weight and shame to him through a false sense of self and based on a sense of unworthiness. Help him disconnect himself and his self-worth from the experiences of life. He is not what happened to him.

"For he is your workmanship, created in Christ Jesus for good works, which you, God, prepared beforehand, that he should walk in them."

May he experience the truth of your word in his life. I pray he knows he wasn't the cause of other's actions. He's your child. Even if other people weren't able to or decided not to value him, he can choose differently now to accept and love himself unconditionally as he is.

God, thank you! I believe you have heard my prayer and will honor it. By faith and the power of the Holy Spirit's intercession with me, I declare it done and so, Amen.

Scripture References:
Matthew 10:27-31, Jeremiah 1:5, Jeremiah 29:11, Ephesians 2:10

23

—

Unhealthy Money Beliefs & Habits

Heavenly Father, purify my future husband's mind of outdated, untrue, or unhealthy beliefs and habits around money he may have inherited from his parents or others who influenced him growing up.

Your word says, "The Lord is my Shepard, I shall not be in want." God, you alone are his Source of everything. I pray my future husband trusts you to supply all of his needs in every area of his life, including material wealth.

You are the God of more than enough and nothing is impossible for you. In you, we lack nothing. Nowhere in your word do you say that money is bad or evil. Instead, you instruct us not to be lovers of money.

"Keep your lives free from the love of money and be content with what you have, because God has said, '"Never will I leave you; never will I forsake you."

Thank you for always being present in my future husband's life. Grow him in wisdom on how to manage his finances so he can do more with what he currently has. Teach him to steward well over what you've blessed him with so far so you can trust him with even more increase in all areas.

I pray he doesn't attach his worth to what he does or doesn't have in material possessions. His life is much more than what he can possess. Give him a spirit of gratitude so he appreciates all he has and attracts more to him as a result.

Break any unhealthy beliefs about him feeling like he has to do everything alone. I pray against him choosing to carry the weight of the world on his shoulders or seeing himself as weak if he asks for help in life.

Unhealthy money beliefs and habits often stem from feelings of unworthiness. God, show your power strong in my future husband's life and realign his thinking with your thoughts that are high above his own with regards to how you value and see him.

Guide him in the steps he needs to take to repair and rewrite his money story, both on a conscious and subconscious level (that usually shows up in his behavior and character over time).

Replace the inaccurate mental images and records that taught him to see everything through the eyes and ears of lack and scarcity. Give him new eyes so he can see his relationship with money in new ways. Money is a tool. A resource. A way to bless others. A tester of character and seed for the Sower.

God, thank you! I believe you have heard my prayer and will honor it. By faith and the power of the Holy Spirit's intercession with me, I declare it done and so, Amen.

Scripture References:
Psalm 23:1, Luke 1:37, II Corinthians 9:10

24

Divine Favor

*D*ear *Heavenly Father*, I pray you'd clothe my future husband in your Divine favor. For whoever finds you, finds life, and obtains favor from you. May your favor protect him throughout his life as a shield and keep him from being negatively affected by life's struggles.

Your word says, "When a man's ways please the Lord, he makes even his enemies to be at peace with him." Let my future husband experience the peace that surpasses all understanding. Make his enemies or anyone or anything that seeks to oppose him, be at peace with him instead.

"Surely you have granted him unending blessings and made him glad with the joy of your presence."

God, your presence is proof of your favor. It is the supreme cause of joy. It's the greatest blessing and the source of all other blessings. May your Divine favor bless my future husband before he realizes his need for it. Go before him and behind him, faithfully protecting and leading him.

I pray your Divine favor would guard my future husband against sickness, isolation, anxiety, attack, and disaster. Continue to bless his life with your favor every day. May he experience your joy, which isn't conditional. Your joy leads him faithfully through pain and marches alongside him in victory.

I pray my future husband lives his life fully in every way because your divine favor reaches far beyond what he visibly needs in this world. Your favor provides comfort, peace, and care for him.

God, thank you! I believe you have heard my prayer and will honor it. By faith and the power of the Holy Spirit's intercession with me, I declare it done and so, Amen.

Scripture References:
Proverbs 8:35, Psalm 5:12, Philippians 4:6, Proverbs 16:7, Psalm 21:6

Coming In Agreement Prayer

*H*eavenly Father, bless my future husband and I with a friendship that is like iron. Let us sharpen each other and build each other up in wisdom and strength for our walk together. I pray we surround ourselves with friends who refuse to gossip, harm their neighbors, or speak evil of their friends.

Bless us with proper discernment regarding choosing friends wisely and having the courage to walk away from friendships that don't serve us. Help us discern love from manipulation and control within our families. I pray for peace regarding all relationships (family & friends) that need to be severed if there is a negative impact.

Heal any deep insecurities within us caused as children while we were in the care of others. Reshape any distorted views we have of ourselves because of these false beliefs.

Continually renew our minds. Correct any false teachings projected on us in the past. Fix any wrong thinking we've developed regarding our beliefs about being loved, safe, protected, and cared for in life by other people.

I pray for Divine healing of past traumas we've experienced. Help us work through any persistent and disturbing responses or repressed emotions that resulted from living through these traumas.

God, I pray we'll pour out our hearts and souls to you, about the things that trouble us the most. May we cast all our cares on you because you care about us, love us unconditionally, and are our safety in this world.

Restore our ability to believe in ourselves fully. Allow us to see ourselves as you created us to be, not the way those caring for us throughout our lives, our communities, culture, or society taught or conditioned us if the influences are unhealthy.

These projections are not our truth. Your word is truth. I speak your word over the scars left by any mishandling of our feelings, bodies, or by us feeling invisible or unworthy.

"The Lord is my Shepard, I shall not be in want." You alone, God, are our Source for everything. I pray we will trust you to supply all our needs, including material wealth. You are the God of more than enough. Nothing is impossible for you. In you we lack nothing. You instruct us not to be lovers of money and not to pursue it at all costs. We will obey you.

Clothe us in your Divine favor. For whoever finds you, finds life, and obtains favor from you, Lord. May your favor protect us throughout our life together as a shield and keep us from being negatively impacted by life's adversities.

Your word says, "where two or more gather together in your name, you are there with them." I come in agreement with my future husband now as we cover ourselves in prayer.

God, thank you! I believe you've heard my prayer and will honor it. By faith and the power of the Holy Spirit's intercession with me, I declare it done and so, Amen.

LOVING EXPRESSION #4

—

Anger

You and your future husband have just had a huge argument. Tempers were high. Communication broke down and you weren't able to get through to him your true feelings and what you really wanted to say. Despite your initial efforts to seek an immediate resolution, you all couldn't find common ground. He's gone out to cool off. You're angry. Feelings of offense and hurt have surfaced for you.

However, you want to convey your anger using loving communication and in a respectful way. Calmly expressing your anger will ensure more anger, resentment, and lasting separation aren't created in your relationship. Using loving communication will help you get through to him and closer to reaching a state of harmony again within your relationship.

Part 1: Written Love Note

Take your dedicated journal and write your future husband a love note expressing your anger using loving communication. Keep the following things in mind with this note. 1. Confess your anger & the cause. 2. Be honest about how you feel. 3. Explain any changes in your behavior resulting from anger. 4. Express any boundaries needed going forward. 5. Actually, make sure your anger is about what's happening in the moment and not about other things. 6. Share ideas on ways you can work together to release feelings of frustration and hurt in healthy ways.

What issues would cause you to feel angry and upset and to have you feeling the ways I mentioned above?

Go into detail about what you'd say to him. Include how you would react to the situation physically. What would your body language be like? How would your face be? Would you be open to him wanting to console or comfort you by showing his affection? Would you openly show your emotions, or would you erect a wall to hide behind? Let it play out in as much detail as possible. It may be uncomfortable, but this is such an important exercise because it'll help you patch things up faster in real life.

Here are some phrases you can use to get you started thinking about how you'd like to express yourself and what you'd like to say, in your own words, to express your anger using loving communication.

Loving Expressions

I'm angry because...	I value your feelings also.
What you said/did hurt me.	I don't want to argue.
We can figure this out.	I want to listen to you also.
I love you.	Let's work together to...
Let's be calm & respectful.	We can get better...

Part II: Spoken Love Note

After you've gotten your words together and know what you want to say to express your anger in a loving way, take your letter and read it out loud as if you are speaking directly to your future husband. Imagine he's there, standing or sitting in front of you. Visualize the experience and feel all the feelings you might feel in the moment.

Allow yourself permission to be you. If you struggle with confrontation or observe that you are uncomfortable with the process, no worries. You can explore this later. It's never fun or comfortable when you are at odds with someone you love. However, this is why practicing loving communication is so important. It will reduce the time it takes you to mend and get back to peace and harmony with each other.

Specifically, for this exercise and note, the spoken portion is extremely important to do because it'll help bring up other situations, experiences, or people who you might still need to forgive and release. Pay close attention to how you feel while doing this exercise.

Things to Remember

#1: Loving communication is going to be an important part of the success of your future marriage. It's even more important when you aren't feeling very loving in the moment. Practicing it in all situations will make you better at doing it.

#2: Anger is a completely healthy human emotion. It's not unhealthy to feel anger. It can even be useful if you know how to use it. It's only if you use your anger in destructive and harmful ways toward yourself and others that it becomes unhealthy. Learn to use your anger constructively, as a tool to strengthen boundaries and let you know what matters to you.

#3: Men need to know in real time what they did to offend you and the results of their actions. Clear communication is essential. "I am angry because..." Starting with this sentence is not name-calling, placing blame, or attacking him. You're owning your feelings. You're respectful and loving, helping him better understand you. This gives him a chance to take responsibility for his own actions and feelings. This way he can change or correct course more quickly and harmony can be restored.

Selah {Pause}

Again, pause here. Check in with yourself. How are you feeling? What things came up for you during this last set of prayers? Was it difficult to express your anger in a loving way? Did you experience any blocks while writing your note or saying it?

How has this group of prayers changed how you're thinking about your future husband as a human being and the things he might deal with in life and in his personal walk with God?

It's time to go back through the previous group of prayers and pray them over yourself. Change out the pronouns he, him, etc. Put me, myself, and I in their place. Focus on the below themes.

Your Friendships + Family Ties
Your Deep Insecurities
Healing Past Traumas
Healing Feelings of Unworthiness
Unhealthy Money Beliefs & Habits
Divine Favor

Take your time as you pray over yourself with this set of prayers. The themes are very important because they deal with the past and the negative effects the past usually has on our present. Spend some extra time here if needed for both the benefit of him and you.

"Your past is a place to be learned from.
Not a place to be lived in."
Robert Sharma

Talking Points & Insight

Use this space to note things that came up for you that you want to work through or revisit later to gain clarity or peace on.

Talking Points for You & God:

1.

2.

3.

Talking Points for You & a Trusted Friend or Professional:

1.

2.

3.

Talking Points for You & Your Future Husband:

1.

2.

3.

Insight Gained

_____

_____

_____

_____

_____

_____

_____

_____

_____

Vulnerability as Power

The word vulnerable comes from Latin and means 'wounding.' Emotional vulnerability is being willing to show emotion, address and share your own emotions, or to allow one's weaknesses to be seen or known; permitting the risk of being emotionally hurt by another.

The foundation for open communication involves honesty, trust, and vulnerability. Unfortunately, in western culture, the word is associated with weakness, the absence of strength, and something that is regarded as not being desirable.

Yet, learning how to be vulnerable in your relationships can fuel stronger, healthier, and more meaningful bonds than perhaps you've ever imagined possible. When you choose to be vulnerable within your relationships and let your guard down, you're able to connect in a raw and open manner. It shows your courage to own your emotions instead of deflecting, avoiding, or denying them. This is very powerful.

Healthy relationships require that we learn how to open up and share from our hearts. You have to be able to listen to your partner and be open to being affected by their words and their feelings, even when it's difficult or painful.

Vulnerability is not a weakness. It's actually a strength that requires confidence in yourself and your ability to embrace challenging situations. It requires you to be connected to how you process emotions and express thoughts and feelings to your partner openly and honestly.

Yes, opening yourself up to vulnerability also means opening up to the possibility of getting hurt. However, it's essential if you desire to feel and experience deep intimacy with your future husband.

As you continue this 40-day prayer journey, really begin to be open and honest with yourself first, then with God about the way you view vulnerability and whether you've closed yourself off to it, in the name of protection.

Remember, walls can protect for a time in a season. But then become barriers for new things to enter out of that season.

God already knows the truth about the unspoken feelings you might carry. But before you'll be truly ready to receive the man God has for you, your future husband, and your happily ever after, you'll need to fully embrace vulnerability as power.

You'll need to re-learn how to be vulnerable and move beyond fear and past pain and be willing to open your heart again. You'll need to learn how to trust someone else with the intimate parts of your heart.

Alone and in God's presence, I feel, is the safest space for you to practice this. Getting practice in before actually needing to do it IRL means you can build up more confidence in your ability to be vulnerable again. What causes you the greatest resistance is usually what you actually need the most. What you don't face, continues to grow in the background.

When you've created a habit of avoiding or burying your emotions, you lose sight of how you actually feel. This causes unnecessary frustration and can turn into shame and self-hatred. Knowing who you are and why you are that way creates better mental and emotional health. You learn self-awareness by allowing yourself to be open and honest about your feelings and the experiences that caused them. You develop immense courage and strength as a result.

It's time to transform your relationship with the idea of vulnerability by embracing it as a positive and powerful tool you can use to fuel greater connection within your relationships, including the one with your future husband.

Self-Reflection: Going Inward

Do I think being vulnerable is a negative or positive trait? Why do I feel this way?

_____

_____

_____

Am I willing and able to articulate my emotions? Do I openly express my feelings in real time whether positive or negative?

_____

_____

_____

Do I currently have at least one person in my life I feel comfortable being vulnerable with? If so, who? How did I establish that level of trust with them?

_____

_____

_____

Have I ever been completely vulnerable in my relationships, romantic, platonic, or family? Why or why not?

_____

_____

_____

Do I feel comfortable expressing positive and loving behavior outwardly in my relationships and everyday life? Why or why not?

_____

_____

_____

What is my love language? What do I need in order to feel loved and connected to someone?

_____

_____

_____

Scripture Meditation #5

"Don't worry about anything; instead, pray about everything.
Tell God what you need and thank him
for all he has done.
Then you will experience God's peace, which exceeds anything
we can understand. His peace will guard your hearts and
minds as you live in Christ Jesus."
Philippians 4:6-7

25

His Character & Integrity

*D*ear *Heavenly Father*, let everything my future husband does set an example for others because he does what is good. Help him show integrity, honesty, and wisdom that cannot be attacked. Let those who oppose him be ashamed because they have nothing bad to say about him.

God, help my future husband walk before you faithfully, with integrity of heart and uprightness. Keep him from following wicked paths that leave him exposed. Instead, fill him with honor and keep his walk safe.

Be a shield to him. Strengthen his character so his mental and moral qualities are in line with your word and instructions for how he should live his life. Grant him a treasure of common sense and help him have a good character.

Lord, let integrity and honesty protect him, for he puts his hope in you. Your word says, "What is desired in a man is steadfast love, and a poor man is better than a liar."

I pray my future husband will be a man who can love faithfully and loyally and who can do so consistently over time, which is how trust and success in anything are created and measured.

God, thank you! I believe you have heard my prayer and will honor it. By faith and the power of the Holy Spirit's intercession with me, I declare it done and so, Amen.

Scripture References:
Titus 2:7-8, I Kings 9:4, Proverbs 10:9, Proverbs 2:7, Psalm 25:21, Proverbs 19:22

26
—

Unwavering Faith

Heavenly Father, I pray my future husband has unwavering faith and that he places complete trust and confidence in you and your word. May he believe sincerely, without doubt or hesitation, you exist.

Your word says, "And without faith, it is impossible to please God, for whoever would draw near to God must believe that he exists and that he rewards those who diligently seek him."

Help my future husband model the people in the bible who gained their good reputations for their acts of faith. God, help him draw nearer to you and strengthen his faith every day. Help him accomplish things he thought were previously impossible, for nothing is impossible for you.

I pray he's already developed a healthy ability to live by faith and not by sight. I pray he also knows that faith without works is dead. Make him a person who is justified by his works and not by faith alone.

Give him a desire to stay meditating on your word because faith comes by hearing, and hearing through the word of God.

Help him realize it is by your grace that he's saved through faith. And this is not from his own doing; it is a gift from you, God, not a result of works, so that he has no reason to boast about it.

I pray his life shows his unwavering faith by what he does. Honor his faith with answered prayers, Divine favor, and abundance, all the days of his life.

God, thank you! I believe you have heard my prayer and will honor it. By faith and the power of the Holy Spirit's intercession with me, I declare it done and so, Amen.

Scripture References:
Hebrews 11:1,6, Ephesians 2:8-9, Romans 10:17, James 2:18

27

—

His Words & Speech

*H*eavenly Father, I pray my future husband has a good command over his speech and knows how to communicate his thoughts and feelings with kindness and love.

Your word says, "Do not let any unwholesome talk come out of your mouths, but only what is helpful for building others up according to their needs, that it may benefit those who listen."

I pray he uses his words to build others up. Help him avoid all perverse talk and to stay away from corrupt speech. Let him speak not in words taught by human wisdom, but in words taught by the Spirit, explaining spiritual realities with Spirit-taught words.

I pray he doesn't have a short temper that stirs up conflict. Instead, make him a patient man that calms disputes. Keep him from too much talk, for it can lead to sin. Help him be sensible and keep his mouth shut when needed.

God, keep my future husband's mouth free from foul or abusive words that seek to destroy peace and harmony in his inner and outer worlds. Your word says, "Gracious words are like a honeycomb, sweetness to the soul and health to the body." May his words always be lined with grace and sweet to those who hear them.

God, thank you! I believe you have heard my prayer and will honor it. By faith and the power of the Holy Spirit's intercession with me, I declare it done and so, Amen.

Scripture References:
Ephesians 4:29, Proverbs 4:24, I Corinthians 2:13,
Proverbs 15:18 & 10:19 & 16:24

28

Leadership Qualities

Dear Heavenly Father, I pray my future husband has excellent leadership qualities. Help him influence and serve others out of Christ's interests in their lives, so they can accomplish your purposes for them. May he treat others the same way he wishes for them to treat him. By doing so, he'll be honoring your word, which says, "Let each of you look not only to his own interests but also to the interests of others."

Being a good leader means he needs to have patience, a spirit of cooperation, love, and modesty. Make him an example for others to follow and not unpleasant or bossy.

I pray he has an upright heart so he can lead others and guide them with a skillful hand. Give him the wisdom and desire to want to develop and improve. By doing so, he will grow in the things of you and positively affect those around him.

Use him to motivate others in line with their higher purposes. I pray his faith will show in everything he does. May he show courage and wisdom when he makes decisions and in his actions.

I pray you'd add all these leadership skills and more to him as a man and as the leader of our future household. Teach him how to be accountable to you for all his thoughts and actions. Because he has this knowledge, may he always seek to please you in how he leads himself and others in his life.

God, thank you! I believe you have heard my prayer and will honor it. By faith and the power of the Holy Spirit's intercession with me, I declare it done and so, Amen.

Scripture References:
Philippians 2:4, I Peter 5:3, Psalm 78:72, Luke 6:31

29

His Preparation

*D**ear Heavenly Father*, I pray you'd prepare my future husband for becoming a husband. I pray he aims to be trustworthy and above reproach. The husband of one wife, sober-minded, self-controlled, respectable, hospitable, able to teach, not a drunk, not violent but gentle, not quarrelsome, and not a lover of money. Teach him how to manage his own household well, with all dignity.

God, increase in all areas of his life, while he decreases. Shape him into the man that possesses the qualities of the husband you designed him to be. Teach him how to take care of the things you will put under his care once he marries and starts a family.

Instruct him in your ways so he knows what it means for him to be a husband as you have commanded and intended it to be and not by the standards of how the world teaches men to behave or live. I pray he seeks your counsel in all matters of the household, finances, and our future marriage.

Teach him how to prepare his heart for oneness. Allow your tenderness in him to be evident throughout our union. I pray he is always open to your instruction and correction over his life, heart, mind, and actions so that it will go well with him for all the days of his life. Shower him with divine favor and keep his ways straight while he waits for us to meet.

God, thank you! I believe you have heard my prayer and will honor it. By faith and the power of the Holy Spirit's intercession with me, I declare it done and so, Amen.

Scripture References:
1 Timothy 3:1-7, John 3:30

Coming in Agreement Prayer

Heavenly Father, teach my future husband and I how to conduct our lives in all honesty, trustworthiness, and with strong moral principles. Help us to conduct ourselves with all humility, gentleness, and patience as an act of worship to you, God. I pray for a spirit of togetherness in my future marriage with my future husband.

I pray we will live our lives by faith. We'll trust in you completely without wavering and know that you are with us every step of the way. I pray we'll always put our hope, trust, and confidence in you.

Lace our words and speech with both kindness and the unconditional love that is found only through our relationship with you, God. Help us to always attempt to protect the unity of the Spirit with the peace that ties us together through the words we speak to ourselves and each other. Let us be slow to anger and quick to seek reconciliation and forgiveness for one another.

God, give us eager hearts to do your will. Give us spirits of obedience and the humility to be servant leaders to each other and in all the areas we have influence. Help us stay focused on your will and vision for our lives as individuals and as a married couple so we can experience lasting success.

God, teach us how to prepare our hearts for oneness within our future marriage. Allow your tenderness to be evident throughout our union. May we always be open to your instruction and correction over our lives, hearts, minds, and actions, so that it will go well with us always. Keep our ways straight while we wait to meet each other in your perfect timing.

Your word says, "where two or more gather together in your name, you are there with them." I come in agreement with my future husband now as we cover ourselves in prayer.

God, thank you! I believe you've heard my prayer and will honor it. By faith and the power of the Holy Spirit's intercession with me, I declare it done and so, Amen.

LOVING EXPRESSION #5

—

Forgiveness

Your future husband has offended and hurt you. You've expressed your feelings to him using loving communication. He has apologized and taken responsibility for hurting you. You all have talked it through and taken other steps to come back together, intending to move forward in your relationship.

However, in order to move forward and not harbor anger or resentment, you'll need to decide to forgive him in your heart and continue to forgive him until you no longer feel emotionally wounded by the hurt. Forgiveness is a choice you'll need to make repeatedly throughout your future marriage.

Part I: Written Love Note

Now, take your dedicated journal and write your future husband a love note forgiving him. Keep the following things in mind with this note. 1. Acknowledge the hurt itself. 2. Be honest about how it affected you and made you feel. 3. Explain any changes in your behavior resulting from his actions. 4. Express any boundaries that need to be put in place going forward. 5. Actually tell him you forgive him. 6. Share ideas on ways you can work together to help you both feel safe in the relationship again and to release the hurt caused in healthy ways.

What kind of things would cause you to feel hurt and to have you feeling the ways I mentioned above?

Go into detail about what you'd say to him. Include how you would react to the situation physically. What would your body language be like? Would you be open to him wanting to console or comfort you by showing his affection? Would you openly show your emotions, or would you erect a wall to hide behind? Let it play out in as much detail as possible.

Here are some phrases you can use to get you started thinking about how you'd like to express yourself and what you'd like to say, in your own words, in your forgiveness love note.

Loving Expressions

I forgive you.	We need to improve...
I won't hold onto...	I love & value myself.
Please do better.	This is how I need love...
I love you.	Let's end old cycles.
Going forward I need...	Let's work together to...

Part II: Spoken Love Note

After you've gotten your words together and know what you want to say in your forgiveness note, I want you to take your letter and read it out loud as if you were speaking directly to your future husband. Imagine he's there, standing or sitting in front of you. Visualize the experience and feel all the feelings you might feel in the moment.

The spoken portion is extremely important to do because it'll help bring up other situations, experiences, or people who you might still need to forgive and release.

Pay attention to how you feel while doing this exercise. Allow yourself permission to be you in whatever expression that needs to be. If you shut down or observe yourself having reservations about the process, no worries. You can explore this more later.

Things to Remember
#1: Forgiveness is for you, not the other person.

#2: Forgiveness doesn't excuse the actions of the other person. Nor does it invalidate your feelings or how their actions made you feel.

#3: Men need to know immediately (when the offense actually takes place) the results of their actions. When you're able to communicate in a clear and concise manner without attacking him or adding trumped-up offenses to the current one, it helps him understand you better. This way he can change or correct course more quickly and reconciliation has the chance to happen sooner.

He won't want to cause hurt and pain for you. Seeing you unhappy or hurt will crush a man who genuinely loves and cares about you, which will be the case with your future husband.

However, he'll need to know specifically what you are feeling and the true consequences of whatever the behavior is. So, yes, it's a BIG deal to make sure he knows the six things I pointed out to include in your forgiveness letter. Only you can teach him how you need to be loved!

Selah {Pause}

Again, pause here. Check in with yourself. How are you feeling? What things came up for you during this last set of prayers? Was it difficult to express your forgiveness? Did you experience any blocks while writing your note or saying it?

How has this group of prayers changed how you're thinking about your future husband as a human being and the things he might deal with in life and in his personal walk with God?

It's time to go back through the previous group of prayers and pray them over yourself. Change out the pronouns he, him, etc. Put me, myself, and I in their place. Focus on the below themes.

Your Character & Integrity
Unwavering Faith
Your Words & Speech
Leadership Qualities
Your Preparation

Take some time and reflect on where you are in your walk with God. Do you usually practice forgiving others? How about forgiving yourself? How can the above areas (if not properly developed) have a positive or negative effect on your relationship with your future husband and in your future marriage?

"The spiritual journey is the unlearning of fear and the acceptance of love."
Marianne Williamson

Talking Points & Insight

Use this space to note things that came up for you that you want to work through or revisit later to gain clarity or peace on.

Talking Points for You & God:

1.

2.

3.

Talking Points for You & a Trusted Friend or Professional:

1.

2.

3.

Talking Points for You & Your Future Husband:

1.

2.

3.

Insight Gained

_____

_____

_____

_____

_____

_____

_____

_____

_____

Marriage as God Designed It

God instituted marriage before there was sin in the world. It was part of His good and perfect plan for humanity, meant to reflect His relationship with His Church and a model that we were to follow.

Marriage, as God designed it, is a creative force. Marriage produces families, homes, and ultimately whole societies. Marriage involves spiritual, emotional, and physical closeness. God meant for married couples to be unified in every way. The foundation of marriage according to God's design is give, not take.

God's intention behind the creation of marriage directly opposes what we've adopted from society's reworking of the institution, which could be the reason it's currently a failing one. It's so important for you to know God's truth and to follow it above all else.

The blueprint for a healthy, whole, happy marriage is one that follows God's design, not the world's. It focuses on serving the needs of another. The original design is not self-serving.

Below are scriptures that give you more insight into marriage as God designed it.

Genesis 2:18 says, "Then the Lord God said, "It is not good that the man should be alone; I will make him a helper fit for him."

"Therefore shall a man leave his father and his mother and shall cleave unto his wife: and they shall be one flesh." Genesis 2:24

"May your spring be blessed. Rejoice in the wife of your youth. She is a lovely deer, a graceful doe. Let her breasts intoxicate you all the time; always be drunk on her love." Proverbs 5:18-19

"He who finds a wife finds a good thing and obtains favor from the Lord." Proverbs 18:22

"An excellent wife, who can find? She is far more precious than jewels." Proverbs 31:10

"House and wealth are inherited from fathers, but a prudent wife is from the Lord." Proverbs 19:14

"In the same way husbands should love their wives as their own bodies. He who loves his wife loves himself. For no one ever hated his own flesh, but nourishes and cherishes it, just as Christ does the church." Ephesians 5:28-29

"Wives are to submit to their husbands and respect them. Husbands are to love their wives in a Christ-like, sacrificial, and humble way." Ephesians 5:32

"Likewise, husbands, live with your wives in an understanding way, showing honor to the woman as the weaker vessel, since they are heirs with you of the grace of life, so that your prayers may not be hindered." I Peter 3:7

"Let marriage be held in honor among all, and let the marriage bed be undefiled, for God will judge the sexually immoral and adulterous." Hebrews 13:4

"What therefore God has joined together, let not man separate." Mark 10:9

Finally, read I Corinthians 7 on your own. I asked this question in an earlier chapter, but it's worth repeating here.

Are you ready to die to your old self? Are you really ready to serve the interests of your future marriage over your own as God designed it?

Scripture Meditation #6

"Have faith in God. I tell you the truth, you can say to this mountain, 'May you be lifted up and thrown into the sea,' and it will happen. But you must really believe it will happen and have no doubt in your heart.
I tell you, you can pray for anything, and if you believe that you've received it, it will be yours. But when you are praying, first forgive anyone you are holding a grudge against, so that your Father in heaven will forgive
your sins, too."
Mark 11:22-24

30

Toxic Culture Influence

Dear Heavenly Father, help my future husband disconnect from all worldly views of what it means to be happy, successful, and valuable as a human being in our society.

Your word says, "For everyone who has been born of God overcomes the world. And this is the victory that has overcome the world—our faith."

God, I pray he will value the things you value. Teach him how to stand his ground against the pressures of toxic social and cultural ways of doing things and living his life. They directly oppose your ways. Instruct him on how he is to live his life according to your will and behave as a man and a husband when the time comes.

Your word says, "For my thoughts are not your thoughts, neither are your ways my ways," declares the Lord. "As the heavens are higher than the earth, so are my ways higher than your ways and my thoughts than your thoughts."

Strengthen my future husband's will, so he measures himself by your standards and not the standards of the world. Grow him in wisdom and discernment so he's better able to perceive people, things, and situations which are dangerous, destructive, or that seek to bring harm to him.

Help him stand guard at all times and be highly selective about what and who he lets into his personal space on a physical, mental, and energetic level. Teach him how to guard all his personal gates so he is better able to withstand temptations that seek to get him off track in life.

You are not a respecter of persons, God, and I pray my future husband follows your example. I pray he stays alert and of sober mind. Help him avoid and resist the attacks of the enemy who prowls around like a roaring lion looking for someone to devour.

I pray in view of your mercy, God, he'll offer his body as a living sacrifice, holy and pleasing to you, this—is his spiritual act of worship. May he no longer conform to the pattern of this world but be transformed by the renewing of his mind.

God, thank you! I believe you have heard my prayer and will honor it. By faith and the power of the Holy Spirit's intercession with me, I declare it done and so, Amen.

Scripture References:
I John 5:4, Acts 10:34, I Peters 5:8, Isiah 55:8-9, Romans 12:1-2

31

FOMO & False Expectations

Heavenly Father, protect my future husband from getting caught in the trap of never being satisfied. Help him resist the urge to chase a false sense of achievement, status, or respect from the world's standards. Shield him from the effects of the fear of missing out, which include anxiety, dissatisfaction, depression, distress, and dis-ease.

You created him to be different. You set him apart. He isn't supposed to fit in. Fear of missing out and distorted realities are the new normal we live in. The belief that other people are living better, more satisfying lives or that major opportunities are being missed, seek to harm his inner peace and joy, which are gifts from you.

I pray against the spirit of comparison, which seeks to rob him of his purpose and personal satisfaction in the gifts, talents, and abilities you've blessed him with. Help him balance being in the world, but not of the world. Keep him in your perfect peace, but not in a bubble of isolation.

For this reason, I pray my future husband will learn how to be content with what he has. Help him keep himself free from being a lover of overindulgence in any area of his life. Ground him in the truth that you will never leave him nor forsake him.

You did not give him a spirit of fear, but of power, love, a sound mind, and self-discipline. I pray he operates from these principles. Allow these truths to cancel out the deception and destruction that the illusion of unquenchable desires seek to bring in his life. He can find everything he truly needs in you.

Your word says, "Why spend money on what is not bread, and your labor on what does not satisfy? Listen, listen to me, and eat what is good, and you will delight in the richest of fare."

God, thank you! I believe you have heard my prayer and will honor it. By faith and the power of the Holy Spirit's intercession with me, I declare it done and so, Amen.

Scripture References:
Hebrews 13:5, Isiah 55:2, 2 Timothy 1:7, John 17:14-17

32
—

Overcoming Fear & Negativity

Heavenly Father, I speak against the spirit of fear, discouragement, and negativity where my future husband is concerned. Let his heart not be troubled or afraid. Let the everlasting peace that comes from you overtake him in every area of his life, so he knows it's of you and not of the world.

Let your presence always be with him everywhere he goes and in everything he does. He can do all things through you who give him strength. I pray he follows your instructions and will let faith, hope, and love lead and guide his life.

God, give him rest in you when he gets down on himself about things that are outside of his control.

Your word says, "Fear not, for I am with you; be not dismayed, for I am your God; I will strengthen you, I will help you, I will uphold you with my righteous right hand."

I pray against the tendency for negativity to creep into his life and become a state of mind that keeps him from believing in miracles, signs, and wonders, which are blessings and a part of Kingdom living.

Your word says, "Without faith it is impossible to please God. Because those who come to you must believe you exist and reward those who earnestly seek you."

I pray my future husband always turns to you when the difficulties of life cause him to develop negative patterns of thinking, cause discouragement, or cause him to become cynical. These states make him lose sight of you and your promises, God. They also seek to damage his faith.

Your word encourages him, "It is for freedom that Christ has set us free. Stand firm, then, and do not let yourselves be burdened again by a yoke of slavery."

God, you called my future husband to be free. I pray he'll sustain his freedom in you. Bless him with the fruits of the Spirit, which are love, joy, peace, forbearance, kindness, goodness, faithfulness, gentleness, and self-control.

God, thank you! I believe you have heard my prayer and will honor it. By faith and the power of the Holy Spirit's intercession with me, I declare it done and so, Amen.

Scripture References:
John 14:27, Isaiah 41:10, Exodus 33:14, Galatians 5:22-23

33
—

Unhealthy Distractions & Behaviors

Heavenly Father, keep my future husband free from escapist habits. Help him to not get lost or trapped in unhealthy distractions and behaviors. I pray he rejects the desire to set his mind on and live his life according to the flesh. Instead, I pray he is a man who sets his mind to live his life by the Spirit.

Your word instructs, "For to set the mind on the flesh is death, but to set the mind on the Spirit is life and peace. For the mind that is set on the flesh is hostile to God, for it does not submit to God's law; indeed, it cannot. Those who are in the flesh cannot please God. For if you live according to the flesh you will die, but if by the Spirit you put to death the deeds of the body, you will live."

I pray my future husband puts to death everything that belongs to his earthly nature: sexual immorality, impurity, lust, pornography, addictive behaviors, excessive social media use, video gaming or VR play, evil desires, overthinking, any type of substance abuse, and greed, which is idolatry. None of these things offer any lasting benefit to him.

Your word warns, "Because of these, the wrath of God is coming."

Fill his life with good things and great people who add to his happiness and fulfillment. This way, he doesn't have to escape his reality using things that subtract from his life energy and rob him of his overall will to fully live.

God, help him rid himself of all such things as these: anger, rage, malice, slander, and filthy language from his lips. I pray evil doesn't overcome him, but he overcomes evil with good.

Your word teaches, "Do not lie to each other, since you have taken off your old self with its practices and have put on the new self, which is being renewed in knowledge in the image of its Creator."

God, thank you! I believe you have heard my prayer and will honor it. By faith and the power of the Holy Spirit's intercession with me, I declare it done and so, Amen.

Scripture References:
Romans 8:5-8 & 13, Colossians 2:5-10, Galatians 5:16,
Romans 12:21

34

A Healthy Ego & Boundaries

*D*ear *Heavenly Father*, bless my future husband with a healthy sense of who he is and who you created him to be. But let him not think more highly of himself as to deceive himself and be puffed up with conceit or pride, which doesn't align with your will for his life.

Your word says, "Do not think of yourself more highly than you ought, but rather think of yourself with sober judgment, in accordance with the faith God has distributed to each of you. For just as each of us has one body with many members, and these members do not all have the same function, so in Christ, we, though many, form one body, and each member belongs to all the others. We have different gifts, according to the grace given to each of us."

Increase my future husband's self-knowledge so he knows how to create healthy boundaries around how he needs to be treated and loved by other people. Change how he thinks about himself in relation to others if he suffers from a distorted view or has forgotten his natural strengths and abilities.

Your word says, "Pride goes before destruction, and a haughty spirit before a fall. The reward for humility and fear of the Lord is riches and honor and life."

I pray my future husband can reap the reward that comes with him operating from a place of humility. God, help him not to see humility as a weakness or a reason for him to let others walk over him or treat him with disrespect or disregard.

Raise him up to be a man after your own heart and show yourself mighty in his life so that people will show reverence to you because of him.

God, thank you! I believe you have heard my prayer and will honor it. By faith and the power of the Holy Spirit's intercession with me, I declare it done and so, Amen.

Scripture References:
Romans 12:3-6, Proverbs 16:18 & 22:4

35
—

Pure Thoughts & Right Actions

*D*ear Heavenly Father, I pray my future husband draws near to you, so you will draw nearer to him. Cleanse his hands of sin, purify his heart, and rid him of any double-mindedness.

I pray he won't simply listen to or read your word, but that he also desires to do what it says and to live his life according to it. Otherwise, he is only fooling himself and won't be able to sustain living a righteous life.

Your word teaches, "If anyone, then, knows the good they ought to do and doesn't do it, it is a sin for them. The thoughts of the wicked are an abomination to the Lord, but gracious words are pure."

Right actions follow right thoughts. Bless my future husband with thoughts that are like yours, God.

"My thoughts are nothing like your thoughts," says the Lord. "And my ways are far beyond anything you could imagine."

Help my future husband restrain from acting outside of your will for his life or doing anything that would cause him to fall out of righteous living.

Bless him with the wisdom from above because it is first pure, then peaceable, gentle, open to reason, full of mercy and good fruits, impartial, and sincere.

Your word says, "Finally, brothers, whatever is true, whatever is honorable, whatever is just, whatever is pure, whatever is lovely, whatever is commendable, if there is any excellence, if there is anything worthy of praise, think about these things."

God, thank you! I believe you have heard my prayer and will honor it. By faith and the power of the Holy Spirit's intercession with me, I declare it done and so, Amen.

Scripture References:
James 4:8,17, Isaiah 55:8, James 3:17, Proverbs 15:26, James 1:22, Philippians 4:8

Coming in Agreement Prayer

*D*ear Heavenly Father, give my future husband and I, spirits of obedience and the humility to follow your word and will in all areas of our lives. Help us reject worldly or cultural influences.

Help us disconnect from worldly and materialistic views of what it means to be happy, successful, and valuable as human beings.

Your word says, "For everyone who has been born of God overcomes the world. And this is the victory that has overcome the world—our faith."

God, thank you for giving us clear instructions for how you purposed marriage and how we should treat each other and operate inside our marriage. Keep the ways of toxic culture influence out of our future marriage.

Give us the endurance and encouragement to walk with the same attitude of mind and heart toward each other that Christ Jesus had toward us, so that with one mind and one voice we may glorify you.

Keep us free from fear, negativity, unhealthy distractions, and behaviors. I pray we'll operate from healthy egos and boundaries with pure thoughts and right actions toward ourselves and each other.

God, you have set us apart and have destined us to be Kingdom dwellers. I pray we will be content with everything we have in life, including our future marriage. I pray we will forego the false expectations of how things "should be" in our marriage and instead we'll do the work to create the marriage we want to be in. It's our responsibility to each other to communicate our needs and desires, then to work together to produce the desired results.

I pray my future husband and I will always put our hope, trust, and confidence in you so that we don't have any reason to be fearful or cynical about ourselves, our marriage, or the world.

I pray we're able to reap the rewards that come with operating from a place of humility before you, God. Help us not to see humility as a weakness or a reason to let others walk over us or treat us with disrespect.

Show yourself mighty in our lives so that people will show reverence to you because of how we live our lives.

I pray we'll draw nearer to you, God, so you will draw nearer to us. Cleanse our hands of sin. Purify our hearts and rid us of any double-mindedness.

Help us to not only listen to or read your word. Also, give us a desire to do what it says and to live our lives according to it. Otherwise, we're only fooling ourselves and won't be able to sustain living a righteous life.

Your word says, "where two or more gather together in your name, you are there with them." I come in agreement with my future husband now as we cover ourselves in prayer.

God, thank you! I believe you've heard my prayer and will honor it. By faith and the power of the Holy Spirit's intercession with me, I declare it done and so, Amen.

LOVING EXPRESSION #6

—

An Apology

Your future husband has just told you that something you said or did hurt him, made him feel insecure, unsure, and discouraged about the relationship. He trusts you enough to open up and be vulnerable with you. He's upset and wants to air things out so that you all can overcome this issue.

You're worried. Irritated. Angry. Regretful. You feel defensive but know you caused the situation to begin with. You decide to trust him with your vulnerability also and use this situation to connect deeper. You need to apologize and also repair any damage done to the sense of closeness and security within the relationship.

Part I: Written Love Note

Now, take your dedicated journal and write your future husband a love note apologizing to him for a mistake you could make or an action that you think might hurt him or undervalue his efforts. Make sure it's heartfelt. It should show you're taking responsibility for your actions and desire his forgiveness using loving expressions that show him it matters to you how your words or actions made him feel.

What kind of action(s) do you think would cause this kind of situation, the feelings I mentioned above, and the need for an apology?

Go into detail about what you'd say to him. Would you still use pet names in this case? Include how you would react to the situation physically. What would your body language be like? Would you go to him and openly show him your affection? Would you become closed off by folding your arms or turning your back? Let it play out and describe it in as much detail as possible.

Here are some phrases you can use to get you started thinking about how you'd like to express yourself and what you'd like to say in your own words in your heartfelt apology love note.

Loving Expressions

I love you.	I value you so much.
Please forgive me.	Let's work at...
I need you.	You matter to me.
We can work this out.	Your feelings are important.
I apologize for...	I want to fix this...

Part II: Spoken Love Note

After you've gotten your words together and know what you want to say to apologize for hurting him, take your letter and read it out loud as if you were speaking directly to your future husband. Imagine that he's there, standing or sitting in front of you. Visualize the experience and feel all the feelings that you might feel in the moment.

If you get choked up, allow it. If tears come, let them. The purpose is to really have the experience in advance so that it's something you can get comfortable doing, feeling, and experiencing repeatedly, until it becomes more natural for you.

This love note is probably one of the most important love expression exercises you'll do in this book. Because it's difficult to express yourself lovingly when things aren't going great or when you've caused the rift. However, this is when it's most crucial. Both parties are their most vulnerable and the risk of damaging things is higher. If you're already even a little skilled at defusing instead of escalating an argument, it'll benefit you not only in your future marriage but in all your other relationships as well.

Things to Remember

#1: You'll need to set aside ego and reasoning in order to be heartfelt and vulnerable. Own your mistakes quickly. The sooner you do, the sooner you get back to happily ever after.

#2: Realize that there are consequences to every action you take and word you speak. Learning to take responsibility for your actions and words will increase your emotional maturity. A high level of emotional maturity is vital to a healthy marriage.

#3: Men have feelings too! Men might not be as vocal about being hurt or show as much emotion as is usually the case for women. However, because this is the case, when he shows you or expresses his emotions, it's not the time to get on the defensive. How would you want to be handled by him if the roles were reversed? You should be able to give the same level of care and love. Including providing the reassurance he needs and a sense of safety when he needs it after there's been a breach of trust.

Everyone needs to be valued and appreciated. So, yes, it's a BIG deal to make sure he knows you are willing and able to make him feel safe in the relationship, the same way you want him to provide that safety and stability for you.

Selah {Pause}

Pause here and check in with yourself. How are you feeling?
What things came up for you during the last set of prayers?
How do you usually handle conflict? Was it difficult to express
a sincere and heartfelt apology? Did you experience any
resistance while writing your love note or saying it?

How has this group of prayers changed how you're thinking
about your future husband as a human being and the things
he might deal with in life and in his personal walk with God?

Go back through the previous group of prayers and pray them
over yourself. Change out the pronouns he, him, etc. Put me,
myself, and I in their place. Focus on the below themes.

Toxic Culture Influence
FOMO & False Expectations
Overcoming Fear & Negativity
Unhealthy Distractions & Behaviors
A Healthy Ego & Boundaries
Pure Thoughts & Right Actions

Take some time and reflect on where you are in your walk with God. How can external influences (if not properly filtered) have a positive or negative effect on your relationship with your future husband and in your future marriage?

"Sometimes our options are the enemies of our peace."
Pastor Steven Furtick

Talking Points & Insights

Use this space to note things that came up for you that you want to work through or revisit later to gain clarity or peace on.

Talking Points for You & God:

1.

2.

3.

Talking Points for You & a Trusted Friend or Professional:

1.

2.

3.

Talking Points for You & Your Future Husband:

1.

2.

3.

Insight Gained

_____

_____

_____

_____

_____

_____

_____

_____

Releasing Selfish Motivations

S poiler alert. Your future husband cannot satisfy you completely. As your husband, it's not his job or responsibility
to do so either. It's also unloving of you to make this a re-
quirement of him.

You might not want to admit it. You might hope this desire
stays a secret buried deep inside of you. Even if this is the case
and you never actually disclose it to anyone, your actions will
tell a different story. With every unmet expectation, you'll
both be deeply hurt. The marriage will start tearing at the
seams. Mounting resentment will follow. Arguments will increase. Disconnection will result. And on and on from there
until you've hurt each other and caused irreversible damage.

Your future husband also won't have magical powers to heal
any of your previous hurts, pains, and disappointments
caused by other people and your own life choices. He won't
be able to fix your life for you. He's also not meant to be a
punching bag for you to take out your frustrations and anger
on.

Reread the above paragraphs again. Selfish motivations will
not help but severely hurt your future union.

Avoid these results by getting real with yourself about your *why*. Learning and aligning yourself with God's design for marriage, which is more about giving than receiving is the key.

In the *Right Intentions* chapter, you went through and hopefully spent some time asking yourself and answering questions about your motivations for wanting to be married and desiring a husband.

Now, it's time to face yourself. You'll need to work to release any selfish motivations connected to your desire to be married. It's time to really get honest about what marriage is and what it isn't based on God's model, not the examples being shown by a toxic society and a traumatized fake reality TV culture.

Get your dedicated journal and take some time now to write out a list of any selfish reasons you had about wanting to be married prior to beginning this prayer journey. Be brutally honest with yourself. You don't need to share this with anyone else, but you also can't afford to not know your truth.

After you have your list, pray about each reason. Ask God to reveal the core issues present. This might take some time, so be open to revisiting this exercise until you've gone over every reason you listed.

Once God shows you the core issues, make a separate list of them. Take each issue to God in prayer. Destroy the paper you wrote your selfish motivations on as a sign of releasing them.

Continue to work with God to heal the core issues so you don't sabotage your future marriage by bringing the baggage of your past into your present and future.

When you know better, you have a responsibility to do better. We need happier marriages. We need to create households for future generations to grow up in that are happy and whole. This way we can properly pour into and take care of each other and any children that will eventually come from our unions. We can't afford to keep adding to the brokenness that is our society now.

It's time for us as individuals to grow up, heal ourselves, and realign to connectedness. By staying committed to this journey, you are contributing to the betterment of not only yourself, but everyone else connected to you, your future husband, marriage, and society as a whole. Thank you.

Scripture Meditation #7

"Again, I tell you this: If two of you agree on earth about anything you pray for, it will be done for you by My Father in heaven. For where two or three are gathered together in My name, there I am with them."
Matthew 18:19-20, NIV

36
—

Grace for Everyday

*D**ear Heavenly Father*, cover my future marriage with your grace for the practical matters of life, my future husband and I will face. I pray we'll always remember to give all our worries and cares to you because you care about us.

Teach us how to balance the pressures of life and the responsibilities of our marriage with grace and steadfast endurance. Grow us in wisdom so we can be good stewards over our marriage and as our family grows to include children, according to your will.

In your word, Jeremiah declares, "Great is his faithfulness; his mercies begin afresh each morning." God, give us the confidence to come boldly to your throne every day. In your presence we know we'll receive your mercy, and will find divine grace to help us when we need it most.

It's your power within us which gives us the ability to free ourselves of old patterns of behavior and ways of thinking that won't serve our union nor honor you. Help us lean on you for direction, God, and not on our own understanding in everything concerning our future marriage. Honor our desire to be good spouses to each other.

Grow and strengthen us daily in and by the grace and knowledge of our Lord and Savior Jesus Christ. And when we feel weak, we'll remember you said, "My grace is sufficient for you, for my power is made perfect in your weakness." As a result, I pray we'll learn to release guilt and shame around our flaws. Instead, we will humble ourselves before you, so that the power of Christ may dwell in us.

Your word says, "where two or more gather together in your name, you are there with them." I come in agreement with my future husband now as we cover ourselves in prayer.

God, thank you! I believe you've heard my prayer and will honor it. By faith and the power of the Holy Spirit's intercession with me, I declare it done and so, Amen.

Scripture References:
*1 Peter 5:7, Hebrews 4:16, Lamentations 3:23, 2 Peter 3:18,
2 Timothy 2:1, 2 Corinthians 12:9*

37
—

Provision Beyond Material Wealth

Heavenly Father, you are Jehovah Jireh. I trust you to supply provision for my future marriage. Align our wills to seek your kingdom, above all else, and to live righteously. As a result, you will supply us with everything we need according to the riches of your glory in Christ Jesus.

Bless us so we live in abundant overflow, allowing us to be a blessing to others. I pray for not only material provision but also abundance and overflow in our bodily health so we can be fruitful, multiply, and live long, active, energetic lives.

Bless us with abundant minds full of creative ideas and strategies that produce new avenues of wealth generation and fulfillment in our lives. Give us favor regarding our relationships. I pray we'll keep company with people that help strengthen us as a couple and who add value and depth to us so we can keep growing and be rich in spirit.

I pray for an abundance of joy, laughter, and healthy curiosity within our future marriage to keep us lively every day. Help us consistently desire to strengthen and grow the intimacy within our future marriage and to draw closer to each other as each year passes.

Your word says, "where two or more gather together in your name, you are there with them." I come in agreement with my future husband now as we cover ourselves in prayer.

God, thank you! I believe you've heard my prayer and will honor it. By faith and the power of the Holy Spirit's intercession with me, I declare it done and so, Amen.

Scripture References:
Philippians 4:19, Matthew 6:33, Philippians 4:13,
II Corinthians 9:8-11

38
—

Patient Love & Communication

Dear Heavenly Father, show my future husband and I, how to exercise self-restraint with how we speak and act toward each other. Teach us how to be even-tempered so we don't go off or shut down in a fight. May we always speak to and about each other with loving words full of life.

You've instructed us on what love is. First, "love is patient and kind." I pray we will act in patient love and kindness toward ourselves and each other all the days of our lives.

Second, "love does not envy, boast, and it is not proud. It does not dishonor others, it is not self-seeking, it is not easily angered, and it keeps no record of wrongs." I pray my future husband and I will honor your word with how we live our lives and show patience and love in our interactions and communication with each other in both good and bad times.

Finally, "love rejoices with the truth. It always protects, always trusts, always hopes, always perseveres." Help us to always be truthful in our future marriage when we communicate. I pray our loving communication will protect our union from outside attacks.

Thank you for giving us words that are like sweet honey to our mouths. Season our words with grace so others will be drawn to your goodness when we tell them about you. Strengthen us so we will not grow weary of doing good, for in due season we will reap if we do not give up.

Your word says, "where two or more gather together in your name, you are there with them." I come in agreement with my future husband now as we cover ourselves in prayer.

God, thank you! I believe you've heard my prayer and will honor it. By faith and the power of the Holy Spirit's intercession with me, I declare it done and so, Amen.

Scripture References:
Psalm 119:103, I Corinthians 13:4-7, Galatians 6:9

39

Forgiving Hearts

Heavenly Father, bless my future husband and I, with hearts of forgiveness. I pray we'll always extend forgiveness toward ourselves and each other and start each new day with a clean slate because love keeps no records of wrongs.

We love because you first loved us. Teach us how to love each other as you love us. Love is not self-seeking. Help us easily and consistently release any offense or hurt caused when we disagree. Establish our future marriage in earnest love, since love covers a multitude of sins.

Bless us with the ability to be kind to one another, tender-hearted, forgiving one another, as you have forgiven us of our sins. I pray we would make it a practice within our future marriage not to go to bed angry and leave room for the enemy to come between us and try to create division in our union.

May you, God, who gives endurance and encouragement, give us the same attitude of mind and heart toward each other that Christ Jesus had toward us, so that with one mind and one voice we may glorify you.

Your word says, "All deeds are right in the sight of the doer, but the Lord weighs the heart." Weigh our hearts and correct us when we are out of line with your word and with doing everything in love, which is how you created us to be and act as your son and daughter.

Your word says, "where two or more gather together in your name, you are there with them." I come in agreement with my future husband now as we cover ourselves in prayer.

God, thank you! I believe you've heard my prayer and will honor it. By faith and the power of the Holy Spirit's intercession with me, I declare it done and so, Amen.

Scripture References:

Ephesians 4:32, Proverbs 21:2, 1 Corinthians 13:4-5,
1 John 4:7-10, NLT, 1 Peter 4:8, 1 John 4:19, John 15:12,
1 Corinthians 16:14

40

Right Timing & Our Happily Ever After

*H*eavenly Father, thank you for your divine timing. You know when it'll be best to bless us with the time of our meeting. Your word teaches us that, "For everything there is a season, and a time for every matter under heaven."

Thank you for taking the lead in our lives while we are single and preparing us for each other in advance, as we seek to live righteously and according to your word.

Bless us with the wisdom to trust in what you have established within us so we can use it in our future marriage. Help us not stray or get distracted by temporary ways to soothe or ease feelings of loneliness and impatience while we're single.

Your word teaches, "Wait on the Lord: be of good courage, and he shall strengthen thine heart: wait, I say, on the Lord."

Give us spirits of heightened discernment so that when we do meet, we will recognize each other as gifts from you. Since you fashioned us with each other in mind, we will complement each other effortlessly. Help us not to only focus on what we see with our eyes but allow us to see each other using our hearts' wisdom as well.

Your word says, "Do not arouse or awaken love until it so desires." I pray we'll trust you to move in our lives and guide us in the steps to take leading to marriage in your right timing without the need to rush.

As a married couple, I pray our first act of submission will be to you, God. You'll be the foundation we build our lives together on. We will trust you to continue to instruct us on the actions we need to take to change our hearts, individually and collectively, as a unit. Help us change any behaviors or wrong thinking that might hinder us from experiencing the fullness of your love or each other's love.

I pray we'll seek your acceptance and approval for how we live our lives, as well as how we love ourselves and each other throughout our future marriage.

Cover us with grace and compassion as we learn to weather the cycles of love, our emotions, varying levels of intimacy, and growing pains. Teach us to respect the ebbs and flows that are a part of nature's natural cycles within our own lives.

Clothe us in humility, so we always seek to give you all the glory, honor, and praise. Let us not lose sight of your power, hand, and love that will allow us to be blessed within our marriage.

I pray we'll recommit, daily, to creating the proper environment and doing the work it takes to maintain our happily ever after, beyond the wedding day, and well into the latter years of our marriage. Help us give up any fantasies or sense of entitlement that makes us think it will just magically happen that way.

Instead, I pray we'll eagerly dedicate our time, talents, and treasure to create our custom happily ever after with equal effort, continuously as we go.

Your word says, "where two or more gather together in your name, you are there with them." I come in agreement with my future husband now as we cover ourselves in prayer.

God, thank you! I believe you've heard my prayer and will honor it. By faith and the power of the Holy Spirit's intercession with me, I declare it done and so, Amen.

Scripture References:
Ecclesiastes 3:1, Song of Solomon 8:4, Psalm 27:14, Acts 10:34

LOVING EXPRESSION #7

Appreciation

Your future husband is everything you prayed to God for.
He's not perfect, but he is a great complement to you. He's
added so much happiness and peace to your life. The fact that
God blessed you with him is reason enough to show him your
appreciation for his being in your life.

No special occasion is needed. You don't want anything. You
simply want to shower him with appreciation in gratitude for
who he is as a person and to you. You are reflective. You feel
very blessed. You want to love on him with words of
affirmation in this moment.

Part 1: Written Love Note

Take your dedicated journal and write your future husband a
love note to show your appreciation for him. You can take
time to reflect on who he is as a person. It's not for anything
he's actually done. Focus instead on just appreciating him for
who he is. Showing appreciation for him lets him know you
value him, that you don't take him for granted, and you're
telling him how you truly feel about him.

What qualities would he possess that would make you appreciative of who he is as a person and have you feeling all the ways I mentioned above?

Go into detail about what you'd say to him. Use pet names if you like. Include how you would react to the situation physically. What would your body language be like? Would you go to him and openly show him your affection? Would you have a Kool-Aid smile on your face? Would he get a massage or cuddle time? Let it play out in as much detail as possible. Experience it in your mind's eye as real.

Here are some phrases you can use to get you started thinking about how you'd like to express yourself and what you'd like to say, in your own words, in your appreciation love note.

Loving Expressions

You're an expression of God's love for me.	I'm blessed to have you.
You fit me perfectly.	You're so impressive.
You are remarkable.	You have a wonderful...
You're such a beautiful man, inside and out.	I love...about you.
	Thank you for Being.
	You take my breath away.

Part II: Spoken Love Note

After you've gotten your words together and know what you want to say to shower him with appreciation, take your letter and read it out loud as if you were speaking directly to your future husband. Imagine he's there, standing or sitting in front of you. Visualize the experience and feel all the feelings you might feel in the moment.

Allow yourself permission to be you. If you feel flirty or giddy, awesome. If you're overcome by emotions at God's faithfulness, own it. The purpose is to really have the experience in advance so that it's something you can get comfortable doing, feeling, and experiencing repeatedly, until the behavior is completely natural for you.

Things to Remember

#1: Smiling will help you really make the feelings more real.

#2: Visualization and spoken word are both powerful manifestation tools to create and bring the things you want into existence.

#3: Men rarely receive appreciation for simply being them! Making it a habit to shower your future husband with appreciation (without it being a special occasion or for something he did) further helps you to elevate yourself in his heart. Whatever way you choose to show your appreciation can further strengthen your bond and help him know you value him as a man.

We all need to be valued and appreciated just for who we are. Men also want to be encouraged to be themselves. Knowing you accept him as he is and aren't trying to change him into someone else will be invaluable to him. He'll know you are a safe space for him to be himself with. This helps to deepen and grow your bond within your marriage.

Again, everyone needs to be valued and appreciated in the moment. So, yes, it's a BIG deal to make sure he knows you appreciate him just for who he is!

Talking Points & Insight

Use this space to note things that came up for you that you want to work through or revisit later to gain clarity or peace on.

Talking Points for You & God:

1.

2.

3.

Talking Points for You & a Trusted Friend or Professional:

1.

2.

3.

Talking Points for You & Your Future Husband:

1.

2.

3.

Insight Gained

_____

_____

_____

_____

_____

_____

_____

_____

_____

Self-Reflection: Going Inward

How has my view of marriage changed since starting this 40-day prayer journey? Am I willing to do the work required to create my custom happily ever after and prepare to receive the marriage God has for me?

_____

_____

_____

_____

_____

What beliefs about marriage do I still need to release for the highest benefit of my future husband and marriage?

_____

_____

_____

_____

_____

Closing Prayer

"The Lord bless you, and keep you
(protect you, sustain you, and guard you);
The Lord make His face shine upon you (with favor),
And be gracious to you (surrounding you with lovingkind-
ness);
The Lord lift up His countenance (face) upon you
(with divine approval),
And give you peace (a tranquil heart and life)."
Numbers 6:24-26, AMP

3 Sample Starter Vows

Your wedding vows are a covenant you'll make to your future husband before God. The vows you all share are binding promises to each other and an agreement that you'll *work together* to reach the loving sentiments and common goals expressed in them.

Here are a few starter vows to inspire you to write your own vows to your future husband. You can continue preparing now to shape the happily ever after you desire.

Starter Vows #1

I want to spend the rest of my days exploring you fully and deeply in every way possible. I always want to be learning you. You came into my life and set my soul ablaze, lighting a fire within that will never be quenched now that it is lit.

Starter Vows #2

You are a miracle to me. Right alignment and timing, our breaths synchronized. Breathing in time with you lets me know that we're more than the love we share. Connected, we're vital to each other's beings. Together with God, we're capable of sustaining each other. I love you with my every-thing. Today I vow to love you for many more of our forever's together.

Starter Vows #3

Please be patient with me. Handle me with care and I'll do the same. We are both fragile and delicate, seeking to be nurtured and held with the utmost respect and tenderness. Shower me with words of life that spring forth from the wells of living water within your heart. Protect me from the elements meant to choke off my growth and vitality. Provide your potent seeds of love for me so that I can bloom to my highest possibilities and potential. Shelter me within the warmth of your love today and always.

BONUS #2

7 Scriptures to Safeguard You

1. "He will equip us with everything to do his will."
Hebrews 13:21

2. "However, as it is written: What no eye has seen, what no ear has heard, and what no human mind has conceived, are the things God has prepared for those who love him."
1 Corinthians 2:9

3. "The Lord watches over you—the Lord is your shade at your right hand; the sun will not harm you by day, nor the moon by night. The Lord will keep you from all harm—he will watch over your life; the Lord will watch over your coming and going both now and forevermore." Psalm 121:5-8

4. "Keep me safe, O God, for I have come to you for refuge."
Psalm 16:1

5. "Do not be anxious about anything, but in every situation, by prayer and petition, with thanksgiving, present your requests to God. And the peace of God, which transcends all understanding, will guard your hearts and your minds in Christ Jesus." Philippians 4:6-7

6. "And we know that in all things God works for the good of those who love him, who have been called according to his purpose." Romans 8:28

7. "Consider it pure joy, my brothers and sisters, whenever you face trials of many kinds, because you know that the testing of your faith produces perseverance. Let perseverance finish its work so that you may be mature and complete, not lacking anything." James 1:2-4

STEPHAN LABOSSIERE

About the Author

Stephan Labossiere is *the* "Relationship Guy." An authority on real love, real talk, real relationships. The brand *Stephan Speaks* is synonymous with happier relationships and healthier people around the globe. For more than a decade, Stephan has committed himself to breaking down relationship barriers, pushing past common facades, and exposing the truth. It is his understanding of REAL relationships that has empowered millions of people, clients, and readers alike, to create their best lives by being able to experience and sustain greater love.

Seen, heard, and chronicled in national and international media outlets including, *The Tom Joyner Morning Show*, *The Examiner*, *ABC*, *GQ*, and *Huffington Post Live*. The certified life & relationship coach, speaker, and award winning, bestselling author is the voice that the world tunes into for answers to their difficult relationship woes. From understanding the opposite sex, to navigating the paths and avoiding the pitfalls of relationships and self-growth, Stephan's relationship advice and insight helps countless men and women overcome the situations hindering them from achieving an authentically amazing life.

Stephan is highly sought-after because he is able to dispel the myths of relationship breakdowns and obstacles–platonic, romantic, and otherwise—with fervor and finesse. His signature style, relatability, and passion make international audiences sit up and pay attention.

"My message is simple: life and relationships require truth. The willingness to speak truth and the bravery to acknowledge truth is paramount." Are you listening? Enough said.

Other Books by Stephan Speaks

The Man God Has for You
www.TheManGodHasForMe.com

Love After Heartbreak, Vol. 1
www.LoveAfterHeartbreak.com

Daily Affirmations for Healing
Love After Heartbreak, Vol. 1 Companion Book
www.AffirmationsForHealing.com

Healing Heartbreak Journal
Love After Heartbreak, Vol. 1 Companion Book
www.HealingHeartbreakBook.com

He's Lying Sis
www.HesLyingSis.com

God Where is My Boaz?
www.GodWhereIsMyBoaz.com

Prayers For My Marriage
www.PrayersForMyMarriageBook.com

He Who Finds a Wife
www.HeWhoFinds.com

How to Get a Man to Cherish You if Your His Wife
www.GetAManToCherishYou.com

How to Get a Woman to Have Sex With You if Your Her Husband
www.BetterMarriageBetterLoving.com